Random House
CABIN FEVER
CROSSWORDS

Edited by
Stanley Newman

Random House
Puzzles & Games

ISBN: 0-8129-3477-6

Random House Puzzles & Games Web site address:
www.puzzlesatrandom.com

Page design and typography by North Market Street Graphics
Manufactured in the United States of America
4   6   8   9   7   5   3

First Edition

SPECIAL SALES

Random House Puzzles & Games books are available at special discounts
for bulk purchases for sales promotions or premiums. Special editions,
including personalized covers, excerpts or existing books, and corporate
imprints, can be created in large quantities for special needs.
For more information, contact Random House Special Markets at 800-800-3246.

1 DANCE FEVER

by Gregory E. Paul

ACROSS

1 IRS employees
5 Clean a chimney
10 Dogie
14 Gap
15 Pet rocks, e.g.
16 Russian city
17 Whit
18 Amber or mastic
19 Casa __ Orchestra
20 '20s dance
22 Actor Sharif
23 Porridge grain
24 Treat with carbon dioxide
26 Kind of drum
30 Colonist William
32 Forster title start
33 '40s dance
38 Ponce de __
39 Sport shirts
40 Sharpen
41 Lively dance
43 United rival
44 Gasp
45 Silver-tongued speaker
46 Part of AWOL
50 Harem room
51 Great Northern diver
52 Ragtime dance
59 Churchill Downs denizen
60 Needle cases
61 Unctuous
62 MA's motto start
63 Breathing sounds
64 Boo-boo
65 Bring up
66 "__ Lady" (Tom Jones song)
67 Gin flavor

DOWN

1 Cartoonist Young
2 Word of disparagement
3 Neighbor of Mont.
4 Char
5 Something very funny
6 Take by force
7 Bridge position
8 Singer Pinza
9 Stadium souvenirs
10 Silver or gold
11 Scent
12 Paul of *Melvin and Howard*
13 Emergency signal
21 Pend
25 Buffalo-to-Rochester dir.
26 #1 on the Mohs scale
27 Chocolate cookie
28 Debatable
29 Nobelist Morrison
30 Oven light
31 Thames town
33 Merge
34 Big bird
35 *A Man for All Seasons* playwright
36 Golden Rule word
37 Accoutrements
39 "The Great Pretender" group
42 ANA member
43 Cart
45 Black Sea port
46 Modify
47 Wilderness Road warrior
48 March man
49 Sign up for
50 Steinbeck characters
53 The 45th state
54 Hold sway
55 Easy throw
56 Lunar trench
57 Mélange
58 Input data, perhaps

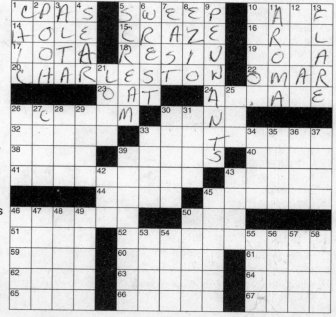

PLAY BALL!

by Rich Norris

ACROSS

1 Cook a soufflé
5 Singer Lanza
10 Strike, in a way
14 Pub quaffs
15 Maine town
16 Dream
17 Hawker's talk
19 A long time
20 Prank player
21 Memorable time
22 Unreconciled
23 Jackal relatives
25 LPGA members
27 Discard
29 RR stop
32 Bed part
35 Slips up
36 Hue and cry
37 A bit: Mus.
38 Hurts badly
40 Gas or oil
41 St. crosser
42 Show's partner
43 They may be loose
44 Classical beginning
45 Place for valuables
49 Word in golf-ball names
51 Stumped
55 Composer Berg
57 Cameroon neighbor
59 Erase, as a computer file
60 Wild pig
61 1978 Jane Fonda film
63 Get some rays
64 Actress Papas
65 In a while
66 Summer drinks
67 Units of force
68 Honeyed drink

DOWN

1 Computer language
2 Texas mission
3 Water spirit
4 Compass dir.
5 Cleaner, at times
6 Songlike passage
7 Campus mil. recruiters
8 Kind of caterpillar
9 Sound of awe
10 Mold
11 1976 sci-fi film
12 Little, for one
13 Kid brother, perhaps
18 Son of Adam
22 Qtys.
24 NFL Hall-of-Famer Graham
26 What we share
28 "Pirate Jenny" composer
30 __ the line (conformed)
31 Leatherworkers' tools
32 Thumb-to-pinky distance
33 Tennis term
34 "The Sign" singers
38 Vegan's no-no
39 *Pilgrim's Progress*, e.g.
40 Sense
42 Exact match
46 Texas/Louisiana lake
47 Makes up (for)
48 Canine feature
50 Songbirds
52 Layer of note
53 Pago Pago locale
54 Use up
55 Palindromic rock group
56 Significant quantity
58 Last word
61 El __ (national hero of Spain)
62 Breakfast side dish

3 THAT'S LIFE

by Randolph Ross

ACROSS

1 Silly look
5 Done in
10 Medium for Marsalis
14 Gold deposit
15 From bad to __
16 Double reed
17 Life, in song
20 Sweet treats
21 Cast off from the body
22 Money rolls
23 Mrs. Cleaver
25 Clunkers
28 Roll-call response
29 New Deal initials
32 You must remember this
33 Fill up
34 *Mask* star
35 Life, to Longfellow
38 First place
39 Facsimile
40 Moon valley
41 Conducted
42 1953-59 French president
43 Smile, in a way
44 Author Grey
45 Humorist Barry
46 Figuring everything
49 Peppy one
53 Life, to Gump
56 "__ Rhythm"
57 Boring tool
58 Air outlet
59 Columbia's parent company
60 Urges
61 911 respondents: Abbr.

DOWN

1 Hefty rival
2 Morning wear
3 Wedding vows
4 Sawyer or Stahl
5 Tarot suit
6 Hits a lazy fly
7 Circle sections
8 Sort-of suffix
9 Social Register word
10 Novelist Amado
11 Rose lover of Broadway
12 Caldwell et al.
13 Love for life
18 Get help from
19 First name of 42 Across
23 Pier
24 Nobel chemist
25 Tag
26 Duck
27 Captured the king
28 On cloud nine
29 Whipper-snapper
30 *Power of Positive Thinking* author
31 Military supplier
33 Struck down
34 Police concern
36 Keynes subj.
37 Nonsense
42 Pasture eater
43 Enjoys every drop
44 Polish currency
45 Prepared potatoes
46 Heron cousin
47 Called off
48 Nerve fiber
49 Corporate identifier
50 Gossiper's nugget
51 Monthly payment
52 Ballpark figs.
54 Put the lid on
55 *Ben-__*

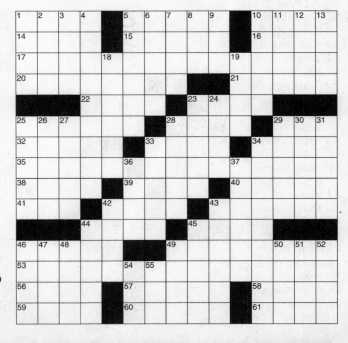

4 WHAT A MESS!

by Gregory E. Paul

ACROSS

1 Attacked
6 Actress Celeste
10 Video medium
14 Caribbean isle
15 Square footage
16 Iroquois Indian
17 Gotten up
18 *Sanford and Son* producer
19 Tick off
20 "We have __ the enemy . . ."
21 Eagles coach, 1941-50
24 Lock brand
26 Greek island
27 Writing pads
30 Marathon trophy
34 Author Dahl
35 "Stormy Weather" singer
38 1969 Peace Prize grp.
39 '40s baseballer Vaughan
40 *I, Claudius* character
41 Off-campus building
42 Sault __ Marie
43 Family member
44 Same
45 Paul Newman role
47 Hose attachment
49 Where to find Aconcagua
52 Court ritual
53 Chicago blues great
57 Alias letters
Something unique

61 Genghis' domain
62 Italy's Detroit
64 Karnak's river
65 Monopoly fee
66 Like a lady of song
67 Mayberry citizen
68 Service club
69 Demurely

DOWN

1 Damage
2 Auto racer Luyendyk
3 Manager of the Giants
4 Actor Vigoda
5 Like some hair
6 Hearty's partner
7 Mountain nymph
8 Charter
9 Crabcake country
10 Singer Brewer
11 Diva's tune
12 Prescription unit
13 Shoe width
22 On a pension: Abbr.
23 Zero
25 Actress Sheedy
27 Riffraff
28 It comes from the heart
29 Doff
31 Eastwood role
32 Make joyful
33 Tesla invention

36 Former CA fort
37 Campanella and Clark
40 Nuts and bolts
41 Product of 62 Across
43 Gainsay
44 Extreme
46 National Leaguers
48 __ favor
50 Studio stand
51 Reek
53 Part of MSG
54 Part of BTU
55 Pickle palace
56 Hash-house sign
58 German city
59 Capp of the comics
63 Card game

5 CLERICAL WORK

by Gregory E. Paul

ACROSS

1 "Get __ of this!"
6 Throws
11 Burst a bubble
14 Oater prop
15 Actor Davis
16 Top card
17 *Life Is Worth Living* host
19 Furrow
20 Ceremony
21 Bridal path
23 Aïda's love
27 Arm art
29 Donizetti works
30 Person from Pago Pago
31 Mental whiz
32 Librarian's device
33 Joker
36 __ Raton, FL
37 Witches' group
38 Richard of *First Knight*
39 __-Cat (Vail vehicle)
40 First state's capital
41 El Greco's birthplace
42 Required
44 Eton's river
45 Cat's __ (living end)
47 Karen of *Little House on the Prairie*
48 Love, to Luigi
49 Appearance
50 Noted diarist
51 *Taxi* character
58 Elephant ending
59 Former Mattel rival
60 Writer Jong
61 Comic Bill's nickname
62 Books
63 Potsdam pistol

DOWN

1 Eur. country
2 My __, Vietnam
3 CIA forerunner
4 Light gray
5 Hotel employee
6 Sells for
7 '75 Wimbledon winner
8 NNW opposite
9 Cravat
10 Boxer, for one
11 George Washington biographer
12 Word form for "eye"
13 "For __ sake!"
18 Diner display
22 Call __ day
23 Former first family of Virginia
24 Cook's attire
25 Football Hall-of-Famer
26 Domingo solo
27 Spud
28 Mass ending
30 Accumulated
32 Peaceniks
34 Soviet co-op
35 Silly ones
37 Musical conclusion
38 Mardi __
40 Bad mark
41 Wide strait
43 Musical sense
44 Genealogy chart
45 Hysteria
46 Organic acid
47 Young women
49 Veal or venison
52 Dutch city
53 Get one's goat
54 Joanne of films
55 Lively dance
56 Frozen dessert
57 Spoil

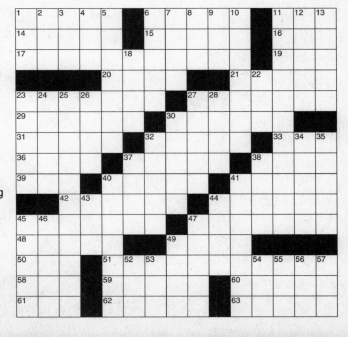

FIND THE ANSWERS

by Dean Niles

ACROSS

1 Singer Falana
5 Follow
9 Apple types
13 Baseball manager Felipe
14 To say nothing of
15 The __ (uneasiness)
17 Clothing catalog
20 Consecrate
21 Evergreen
22 Draftable
23 Singing style
25 Bistro
27 *What's My Line?* highlight
32 Rice-A-__
33 Bubbles over
34 Hooligan, in Britain
37 Draw forth
39 Ember, later
40 Stocking shade
42 Smidgen
43 "__ Romantic?"
46 Harris honorific
47 *Dallas* spinoff
49 Hemingway of *Central Park West*
52 Party with poi
53 "Put __ on it!"
54 NATO counterpart
57 #2 on the hit parade?
61 Trial tactic
64 Medieval strings
65 Actor O'Neal
66 Greek peak
67 "And here it is!"
68 March time
69 Italian painter

DOWN

1 Flowing rock
2 Actor Ken
3 Bonkers
4 Like Hoffman in *Rain Man*
5 Steak style
6 Poetic pugilist
7 "What'd __" (Charles tune)
8 Get the worst of it
9 Beatles' award: Abbr.
10 *Little Women* writer
11 Chili con __
12 Unmitigated
16 Sojourn
18 Fairy-tale beginning
19 Thoughtful
24 Autocrat
26 Aide: Abbr.
27 Vocal horse
28 Skywalker's teacher
29 Cold-shoulder
30 Wind measures
31 Like some battles
34 Cosmonaut Gagarin
35 Welcoming
36 Ice mass
38 __ kleine *Nachtmusik*
41 Paris, vis-à-vis Helen
44 Wise one
45 Firms up
47 Joshed
48 Votes against
49 Teen's hangout
50 Certain Alaskan
51 Western rope
55 Start for culture
56 Area meas.
58 Seine feeder
59 Petty officer
60 __ B'rith
62 "Rose __ rose . . ."
63 Abu Dhabi's federation: Abbr.

7 MATERIALISM

by Norma Steinberg

ACROSS

1 Lazarus or Samms
5 Kiddie-lit elephant
10 Group of wolves
14 Musical Diamond
15 "Now, Pablo!"
16 Monster
17 Barbie, e.g.
18 Do a double-take
19 Spare
20 Daydreaming
23 Like Princeton, as of 1969
24 Behaves
25 Slugger's turn
28 Strainer
31 Sediment
32 Get even for
34 Skiers' meccas: Abbr.
37 Bunny-trail traveler
40 Some coll. students
41 Juan's friends
42 Brown shade
43 Statement of belief
44 Bet acceptor
45 Mule, e.g.
47 Not of the clergy
49 Quarterback great
55 Advise
56 Mrs. Kramden
57 She loved Narcissus
59 Skin-cream ingredient
60 Macpherson or Moss
61 Was sorry for
62 Actress Rowlands
63 Göteborg native
64 Hied

DOWN

1 Howards __
2 Feline sound
3 Venus de __
4 Set aside
5 Cleo's craft
6 In front
7 Gravy holder
8 Eyebrow shape
9 Assess
10 Part of NYPD
11 Go-between
12 Rocky peaks
13 Actor Olin
21 Piece of real estate
22 Poe bird
25 Snakes
26 Row of seats
27 Certain sandwiches
28 "Ready, __!"
29 Long-division word
30 Strong personalities
32 Wile E. Coyote's supplier
33 Vacuum
34 Truck manufacturer
35 Flag
36 Aspersion
38 More unusual
39 Faculty members
43 Eye part
44 "__ the season . . ."
45 Trite
46 Wading bird
47 Spiked
48 Fred Astaire's sister
50 Root vegetables
51 __ hot and cold (waver)
52 Catch a bus
53 ". . . __ of kindness yet"
54 "This is fun!"
55 Droll wit
58 Bet in roulette

8 NONSENSE

by Eileen Lexau

ACROSS
1 Church feature
5 Author Carr
10 Way off
14 Mortgage, e.g.
15 End of a Stein line
16 Swing around
17 Nonsense
19 Confessed to the cops
20 Provided
21 Remodels
23 Small bird
24 Egg-shaped
25 Sir Lancelot rode one
27 Driver's dread
30 Triad, for one
31 Nearsighted toon
32 1/100 of a krone
33 Haws' companions
34 "Close, but no __!"
35 Norse god
36 Clod
37 Dress smartly
38 Some slippers
39 Body's building blocks
41 Passé
42 Unseats
43 Muggy
44 *Hoi __*
46 Jumbo planes
50 Scott Turow book
51 British nonsense

53 To be, in Nice
54 Old calculators
55 Turner of films
56 __ in the Attic (Hellman play)
57 Tangy fruit
58 Part of CBS

DOWN
1 Duke of __ (Portugal conqueror)
2 Chanteuse Edith
3 Women's mag
4 Benefactors
5 Asked for ID
6 Lauder rival
7 Heavy weight

8 Curve
9 Actions
10 Have at
11 Nonsense
12 Polly or Em
13 Rules: Abbr.
18 Bobbled the ball
22 Dimwit
24 Bach's instrument
25 Gather wool
26 Nonsense
27 Green plums
28 Sobbed
29 Barbie's beau et al.
30 Meat cut
31 Bearings
34 Prone to carp

35 Gets a better response than
37 Colombian coin
38 Venomous snake
40 Brides' fabrics
41 He rode the *Beagle*
43 Canned-music club
44 Yeats or Keats
45 Aware of
46 Fall guy?
47 "You __ me!"
48 Long, long time
49 Little squabble
52 Brit. decoration

9 CHURCHGOING

by Dean Niles

ACROSS

1 Reference book
6 Pancake chain
10 False god
14 Slump down
15 Neck area
16 Actor Lincoln
17 American plant
20 Heights of the Mideast
21 Walks heavily
22 __ City, NV
26 TV talker Ricki
28 "__ You Glad You're You?"
29 Hockey great Gretzky
31 Dollop
34 Try again
35 Thin gruel
36 Swiss city
38 With mutual misunderstanding
41 Roof material
42 Not professional
43 Skewed
44 Sucker
45 Become narrower
47 Brink
48 Coyote sound
49 Fish-tank need
50 Fabled fellow
53 Foul-smelling
56 Insanity
62 Phrase of comprehension
63 Lay __ the line
64 Exxon vessel
65 Lean
66 Skunk Le Pew
67 Terminates

DOWN

1 Pt. of speech
2 Syllable to sing
3 __ cit. (footnote abbr.)
4 NASA affirmative
5 Water tap
6 Part of 6 Across
7 Sounds of glee
8 Without shame
9 Zest
10 Ball participant
11 KalKan rival
12 In between
13 Plenty
18 __ compos mentis
19 Maintenance
22 Diamond measures
23 Queen of Soul
24 Porter
25 Harsh sound
27 Full of wrath
29 "We __ robbed!"
30 Delicious, for one
31 Hot spot
32 Settle a score
33 Roasting accessory
35 "Fiddlesticks!"
37 Dynamite inventor
39 Diver's neighbors
40 Former Mideast union: Abbr.
46 Missouri River feeder
47 Rental fare
48 Washed off, in a way
49 Small whopper
50 Wait __ (slow down)
51 Leisure
52 Submachine gun
54 Cut up
55 Painter Magritte
57 __ and tuck
58 Illumined
59 Showman Ziegfeld
60 House mem.
61 Many mos.

10 GOTHAMITES

by Gregory E. Paul

ACROSS

1 Ritz, e.g.
6 Early explorer
10 Secluded valley
14 *Nixon in China*, for one
15 Puerto __
16 Status
17 NYC-born novelist
19 Snorkel's dog
20 Neighbor of Mich.
21 Waif model Kate
22 German
24 Croupier's tool
25 Kestrels and tercels
26 Leatherneck
29 __ Lawrence College
30 "Wellaway!"
31 Budget part
33 Prize endower
37 Remote button
38 Golf great
40 Tom, Dick or Harry
41 Hoard
43 Food shop
44 __ mater
45 Mary I, e.g.
47 Graham's address
49 Pittsburgh gridder
52 Tailless cat
53 Cinema offering
54 Nastase nemesis
55 Sch. auxiliary
58 Limerick's locale
59 NYC-born composer
62 *Ja* opposite
63 Allows to mature
64 Flax fabric
65 Very, in Vichy
66 Time past
67 Something bet

DOWN

1 Sounds of cheer
2 Type of tournament
3 Field house?
4 Be human
5 Nonprofessional
6 Remove
7 Tire mounts
8 Curling surface
9 Name below the title
10 NYC-born comedian
11 Numbers game
12 First name in rock
13 Inert gases
18 Wags
23 Panache
24 NYC-born singer
25 __ *Attraction*
26 Family member
27 Grad
28 Pro __
29 Look of disdain
32 Witch's home
34 Salve
35 Admiral Zumwalt
36 *A Passage to India* director
39 Remove the warhead
42 *Enterprise* navigator
46 Dance club employee
48 Marx colleague
49 Exhausted
50 City on the Moselle
51 Weird
52 Elk kin
54 Remus title
55 Member of the Clinton cabinet
56 Expedition
57 Elizabeth I's mother
60 Alter follower
61 Caboodle's partner

11 BY TH' NUMBERS

by Bob Lubbers

ACROSS

1 Sounds of satisfaction
4 Normandy city
8 Permit
13 French head
15 Mishmash
16 Hotelier Helmsley
17 __ of approval
18 Semis
19 Slangy farewell
20 Last minute
23 In Nod
24 Rip
25 Film buff's cable choice
28 Stuck-up one
30 Ben or Jerry
32 Pigpen
35 Bridal-notice word
37 Background babble
38 Jinxed visitor
43 Fight site
44 Dead or Red
45 Comedian Louis
46 Easy-chair occupant
49 Cartoonist Peter
52 Actor Danson
53 Brainstorm
55 Strain
59 Shakespearean comedy
61 Gene Tierney role
64 Shaver brand
65 Triple-decker cookie
66 Prose commentary
67 Honk
68 Close by
69 Insurrectionist Daniel
70 Finishes
71 Give it a shot

DOWN

1 Perplexed
2 Bounders
3 Madame de __
4 Jubilation T. __ (Capp character)
5 Landed
6 Number on a black ball
7 Snacks
8 Attractive
9 Jet manufacturer
10 Home site
11 It's next to nothing
12 Conflict
14 North Pole workers
21 Poetic contraction
22 Nag nibble
25 Man from Mars
26 Unkempt
27 Greek island
29 Spelling contest
31 Singer Rawls
32 Incite
33 "__ Little Words"
34 Give way
36 USN rank
39 Gene material
40 Airport areas
41 Iced drink
42 Construction workers
47 Dutch commune
48 Compare
50 Sister
51 Heavenly hunter
54 Burns river
56 Plumed fisher
57 Harvest wool
58 Yarn
59 Food server
60 Walked on
61 Brown or Paul
62 Hardwood tree
63 "Made in the __"

by Lee Weaver

ACROSS

1 Boxer's bane
6 Droops
10 Seeks information
14 Flexible
15 Spanish river
16 Lab vessel
17 Aisle escort
18 Jockey's strap
19 Chair or bench
20 Western featuring Elvis
23 Blvd. crosser
24 Marshy land
25 Shoebox letters
26 Raged
28 Actor Astin
30 Jai __
31 Huck's transport
35 Heredity factor
36 Turkish currency
39 Pierre's love
40 Mixes
43 Go it alone
44 Reads, with "over"
46 Ayres or Alcindor
47 Actress Markey
48 Suffix denoting smallness
50 Name for a Dalmatian
52 Vermont-inn sitcom
55 Onassis' nickname
56 Plant pouch
59 Numero __

60 Exodus sign
63 Campus building
65 Poker hand
66 Actress Verdugo
67 Nevada city
68 Fork prong
69 Less civil
70 Reply-requested encl.
71 Rosebud, e.g.
72 Tarot users

DOWN

1 Pat the pillow
2 Cotton thread
3 Patriot Allen
4 "Excuse me!"
5 Regular TV show
6 Bilko's rank
7 Vigoda and Burrows
8 Macon breakfast
9 The *Moonlight*, for one
10 DDE's opponent
11 Pressing need
12 Tart thief
13 Overfilled
21 Necessities
22 Parker House or kaiser
27 Employee's goal
29 Hard stuff
31 Modern music style
32 Latin verb
33 July 4th display

34 Saw parts
37 Boxing great
38 Lawn piece
41 Mended
42 Pledged by oath
45 Try
49 Spews forth
51 Detroit sluggers
52 Subjects for Rubens
53 __ *Gay*
54 Forest path
56 Napped leather
57 Emmy-winner Ed
58 Burns slightly
61 Highest digit
62 *NYPD* __
64 Shemp's brother

13 TRIM-A-TREE

by Diane C. Baldwin

ACROSS

1 Big brass
6 *Amadeus* star
11 Jethro's uncle
14 Small egg
15 Sandwich treats
16 __ Miss
17 *Who's the Boss?* star
19 Peeples of *Courthouse*
20 Like the gray mare
21 Horseshoe pitch
22 More unnatural
24 Be significant
26 Deuce beater
27 Went quickly
28 Appear once again
32 Weaving frames
34 Toe tormentors
35 Sort
36 "__ well that . . ."
37 U of the UN
38 Patch location, perhaps
39 Blanc or Brooks
40 Perjurers
41 Behind bars
42 Doesn't buy
44 Belafonte tune
45 Coat parts
46 Tart apple
49 Pageboy, e.g.
52 Pumice, before cooling
53 TV schedule abbr.
54 Smarts stats
55 *Easter Parade* star
58 Rev, as an engine
59 Grenoble's river

60 Was brave
61 Millinery item
62 Gangster Lansky
63 Apologetic

DOWN

1 WWII Japanese general's family
2 It separates the tonsils
3 "Peggy Sue" rocker
4 Three-time boxing champ
5 Comes to rest
6 *The Planets* composer
7 Author Leon
8 Chair part
9 Logically consistent

10 Respects
11 James or Mitchell
12 Author Wiesel
13 Letter starter
18 Where the "Boyz" are?
23 Cereal grain
25 Uses the crosshairs
26 Aquatic birds
28 Laughs loudly
29 "You're Sixteen" singer
30 Jubilant mirth
31 Stretched the supply
32 Barnyard bleater
33 Sub in a tub
34 Shoots the breeze

37 Tufted songbird
38 *The Court Jester* cutup
40 Conrad novel of 1900
41 False stories
43 Diner or smoker
44 Battle, for one
46 Take the odds
47 Dogpatch denizen
48 Rice field
49 Elevated
50 Greenish blue
51 Ain't proper?
52 Orpheus' instrument
56 Susan of *L.A. Law*
57 7-faced film doctor

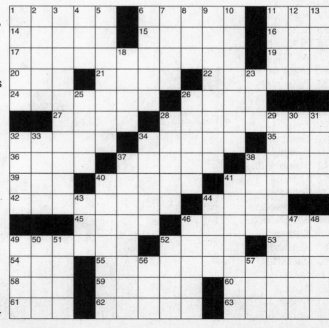

ACROSS

1 State
5 Sp. miss
9 Vanquishes
14 Voir __ (jury examination)
15 Moss or Lorenz
16 Brazilian state
17 Walcott
19 Like a brook's bottom
20 Attended to
22 Match segments
23 Milquetoast
26 Cloudy gems
28 Extreme
29 Write down
31 Disney characters
32 Double agents
33 *Elle*
36 Aleutian island
37 More angry
38 Tyrannical ruler
39 Guided
40 Texas shrine
41 Like bayou cuisine
42 Some autos
44 Actress Dorothy
45 Challenges
46 Baseboard fixtures
47 BLT topper
48 Danish cheese
51 __ Joe (Twain character)
53 DiMaggio
57 Teacake
58 __ breve
59 Projecting point
60 Disreputable
61 Caster's spool
62 Portent

DOWN

1 Pt. of speech
2 Contend
3 Bruin of fame
4 Mideast area
5 Most likely to secede?
6 Indian royal
7 Sulky race
8 Suit to __
9 Small ammo
10 Corrodes
11 Jackson
12 Hues
13 Simon __
18 Gray and Moran
21 Overdoer of a sort
23 Capital of Rio Grande do Norte
24 Wear away
25 Namath
27 __ de deux
29 Models
30 Emulsified spread
32 Gripe
34 Favorite place
35 Flying fishers
37 Trudge in the muck
38 Convince of
40 Ripen
41 Saguaros, e.g.
43 In the neighborhood
44 Ungodlike
45 Bunny hug, for one
46 Room: Fr.
47 Overlook
49 Slightly open
50 Mouse relative
52 *Mrs. Miniver* actor Richard
54 Slim or Diamond follower
55 Single
56 Nighttime, in poems

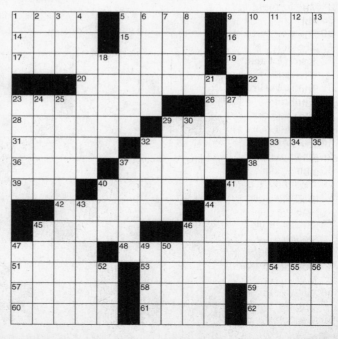

by Gregory E. Paul

ACROSS

1 Avert, with "off"
5 Whitefish
9 Coal slide
14 Inter __
15 Protagonist
16 Cliff dwelling
17 Skating place
18 Part of AKA
19 UMW member
20 Colonial clergyman
23 Patriot Allen
24 Toast starter
28 Dentist's command
32 Bacon serving
33 Colorful pet
37 Big rig
38 Coach Parseghian
39 Beseech
42 Medical aide: Abbr.
43 Ship off
45 Mel Tormé's nickname, with "The"
47 Enrages
50 Patriot Silas
51 Bile acid, e.g.
53 Warren or Joyce Carol
57 Billy Joel album, with *The*
61 Topic for McLuhan
64 Palindromic time
65 Swenson of *Benson*
66 Moon of Uranus
67 Spiffy
68 Earth's inheritors?
69 Equals
70 Countertenor
71 Rochester's beloved

DOWN

1 Mockery
2 Mr. Ness
3 Last inning, usually
4 '60s TV adventure
5 Role for Oland
6 Tiller
7 Bear in the air
8 Stall
9 Tool for Eisenstaedt
10 One with will power
11 Coffeepot
12 Father's Day gift
13 Mountain ending
21 Assured of success
22 That girl
25 Knickknacks' place
26 Cadence
27 Shuttle gasket
29 "Smoking or __?"
30 One-time John Candy series
31 Golden-__ corn
33 Homes: Sp.
34 "__ We All" (1929 song)
35 Hope of Hollywood
36 Marketing start
40 Actress Gardner
41 Domingo, e.g.
44 __ cri
46 British break
48 American Leaguers
49 Part of RSVP
52 Shalala or Summer
54 US Chief Justice, 1836-64
55 Alps peak
56 Plumber's aid
58 Yuletide
59 Application of paint
60 Biblical preposition
61 Glove-box item
62 Before
63 Tool's partner

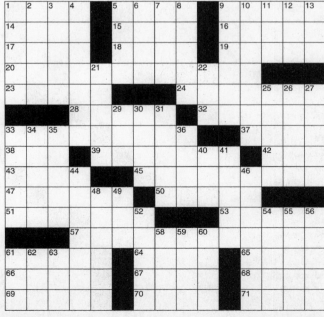

16 SMALL TALK

ACROSS

1 __ avis
5 Russian port
9 Modify
14 Straw in the wind
15 Flag holder
16 10:1, e.g.
17 W.C. Fields' foil
19 Construction-site sight
20 Somebody
21 "We __ Family" (Sister Sledge)
22 Break
24 Fish story
27 Cycle starter
28 "__ De-Lovely" (Porter tune)
29 Bemoaned
34 Moisten the meat
37 Actress Rogers
38 Desiccated
39 "__ a Song Go Out of My Heart"
40 Confronted
41 Former aide Alexander
42 Go out for a strike?
43 Warts and all
44 Annoys, in a way
45 Egg style
47 __ for the course
48 Take first
49 Do recon work
54 Comebacks
58 Excluding none
59 Far from SSW
60 "What's in __?"
61 Albee play
64 Customs
65 On the summit of
66 "__ See Clearly Now"
67 Skew
68 Jonson and Johnson
69 __ up (enlivens)

DOWN

1 Mechanical man
2 Range name
3 Nonconformist
4 Whichever
5 Donizetti works
6 Brown mushroom
7 __-pitch softball
8 Crucial determinants
9 Esoteric
10 *Comic Relief* comic
11 State, in France
12 Nonet count
13 Active guy
18 Coffeehouse choice
23 Dank
25 Winona Ryder movie
26 Brings forth
30 Crooner Ed
31 Hardwood
32 Great Lake
33 BA and MSW
34 Lettuce type
35 Ointment ingredient
36 Attached, in a way
37 Not fem.
40 Hardly audible
44 Zahn of TV
46 Most severe
47 Some jellyfish
50 Church law
51 Like some lager
52 Open, perhaps
53 High schoolers
54 Butts
55 Hydroxyl compound
56 O'Hara's estate
57 Attempt
62 Geologist's suffix
63 Backtalk

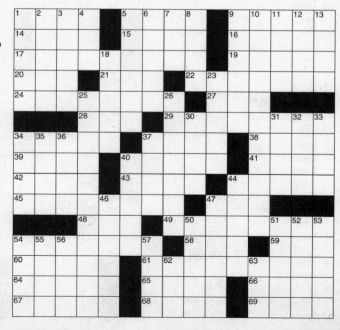

17 FLOWERY LANGUAGE

by Gregory E. Paul

ACROSS

1 Landlocked Asian country
5 Name for a police dog
9 Part of CNN
14 *The Four Seasons* star
15 Raced
16 *The Life of __*
17 Become exhausted, with "out"
18 Jane of fiction
19 Entertain
20 New Hampshire's state flower
23 Curvy letter
24 Barbara and Nathan
25 Pallet
27 Prairie wolf
30 Seedless raisin
33 Tell a whopper
34 Wipe out
37 __ *Frome*
38 __ breve
40 Winter rain
42 Actor Ken
43 Auctions off
45 Peruvian peaks
47 __ de la Cité
48 Nutrition-label listing
50 Quagmire
52 Prosperity
53 Easy __ (simple)
55 Tolstoy topic
57 Loren/Quinn film, with *The*
62 Wear away
64 Thickening agent
65 Verdi villain
66 Borden mascot
67 Singer James

68 Piscator's place
69 *Dead __ Society*
70 Lively dance
71 Art Deco designer

DOWN

1 Reindeer herder
2 Manager Felipe
3 Aroma
4 Greek poetess
5 NFL team
6 Rules man
7 "To __ human . . ."
8 Compost item
9 Cereal sound
10 Prepare to fire
11 With *The*, Raymond Chandler screenplay
12 Subtraction word
13 Peepers
21 Dilatory
22 Tempe sch.
26 "Sock __ me!"
27 Necklace feature
28 Edmonton skater
29 Texas flower of song
30 Acorn, e.g.
31 Exemplars of toughness
32 Meara and Murray
35 First name of 14 Across
36 D.C. legislator
39 *"Der __"* (Adenauer)
41 Secular

44 *The Fighting __* (Wayne film)
46 Evian evening
49 Land of Lincoln: Abbr.
51 Cookbook entry
53 Severe
54 Use a rink
55 Emulate Niobe
56 "Alice's Restaurant" singer
58 Ripening agent
59 Rapunzel's pride
60 "__ Around" (Beach Boys song)
61 Painter Gustave
63 Dah alternative

18 HANKIE PANKY

by Patrick Jordan

ACROSS

1 Ye __ Tea Shoppe
5 Festivals
10 Spheres
14 Early bird's prize
15 Swiftly
16 Breathing sound
17 Codefendant of Leopold
18 Attach, in a way
19 Trojan War hero
20 Quarterback Bart
22 Swiss river
23 Its cover has a red border
24 American game birds
27 Trombone part
28 __ Lingus
29 Jerusalem shrine
33 Former Chinese chairman
36 Print-shop needs
37 Wheat bristle
38 Gull relative
39 Whillikers preceder
40 It's regrettable
44 Haggard heroine
45 Pulls down
46 Riverbank tree
52 Wheel shaft
53 Part of UAR
54 Lake in the Sierras
57 Make angry
58 Cleric's quarters
60 Mah-jongg piece
61 Answered the charges
62 Brought to a halt
63 Flair
64 Clinton and Hatch: Abbr.
65 Prepare for the anthem
66 Challenge

DOWN

1 Fly-by-night group
2 Bandit's booty
3 Fantastical
4 Involves in strife
5 Hiatus
6 Beelike
7 Maui porch
8 Squash variety
9 Westernmost African nation
10 Public speaker
11 Indira's son
12 Culpability
13 Genders
21 Designer Gernreich
25 Animated chihuahua
26 Tierra __ Fuego
27 Fully marbled?
29 Part of Harpo's outfit
30 Brightly colored
31 Gen. Pershing's conflict
32 Abby's sister
33 Transitional word
34 Provides weaponry to
35 Half of 11?
38 Ruby-__ hummingbird
40 Phi follower
41 Changes the title
42 Toothpaste form
43 Popeye or Ahab
44 Exceeds the limit
46 Distorts
47 Napoleon's fate
48 Burstyn or Barkin
49 Bestow
50 *Happy Birthday, __ June* (Vonnegut novel)
51 *Ghosts* playwright
55 Patron saint of Norway
56 Counting-rhyme opener
59 Teacher's deg.

FLORA AND FAUNA

by Shirley Soloway

ACROSS

1 Dawber or Shriver
4 Computer input
8 Actor Lorenzo
13 Winglike
15 Burden
16 "Mighty Lak' __"
17 Spotted flower
19 *Niña*'s sister ship
20 Israeli city
21 Even
23 Short play
24 Open, in a way
26 Shoe soles
28 Putin's domain
31 Battleship shade
32 Shore bird
33 "Santa Claus Is Coming __"
37 WA clock setting
40 Bigotry
41 Sports-car part
42 Crowd sound
43 Pose a question
44 Opera giant
45 Border
46 Ornamental case
48 Formal
50 Shock
52 Pesto ingredient
54 Male moose
55 Plant starter
57 Lamp inhabitant
61 Verbal exams
63 Lawn bane
65 Taylor of *The Nanny*
66 San __, Italy
67 River residue
68 Tropical fish
69 Southwestern Indians
70 Marvin or Majors

DOWN

1 Country walkway
2 *Inter* __
3 Yuletide trio
4 Pt. of a fiver
5 Vocalist Baker
6 Spring blossom
7 "__ sow, so shall . . ."
8 Toddler's perch
9 Grain bristle
10 Tropical trees
11 Moving about
12 Theater units
14 Says "No!"
18 Hindu noblewoman
22 Suburban trees
25 Marsh plants
27 Covered vase
28 Singer McEntire
29 *QB VII* author
30 Windowsill flora
34 __ *Town* (Wilder play)
35 Capote, to pals
36 Some MDs
38 Droops
39 Low card
42 Barn dancers
44 __-de-sac
47 More statuesque
49 Diana of *Mystery!*
50 Scrub a mission
51 Baby food
52 *Chapeau*
53 "There Is Nothing Like __"
56 Light tan
58 Toolbox item
59 Resort spot
60 Spanish compass point
62 Coral or Red
64 Derek and Jackson

by Dean Niles

ACROSS
1 Join, in a way
4 False steps
10 Fight decisions
14 He defeated Spinks
15 Dry gulch
16 "Big Island" port
17 "No __ is an island"
18 Slept noisily
19 Mexican mineral
20 Move back and forth
22 Magical Henning
24 Soon
25 Twelve
27 Dutch airline
30 Music genre
33 Zilch
34 Tic-tac-toe win
35 More drenched
37 Ballroom dance
39 Beat
42 Madison County curiosities
44 Tolerate
45 Shock to the system
47 Imprison
48 Nothing but
50 Family member
54 Math. course
55 Actor Delon
57 Synagogue scroll
58 Pigeon
60 Monotonous

63 Off base?
65 Medicinal legume
67 Usurer's charge, for short
68 Mass. neighbor
69 Hooky player
70 Wriggly fish
71 Forum wear
72 Regarded to be
73 Compass dir.

DOWN
1 Chinese boat
2 Tennyson character
3 Separate
4 Pant
5 Cartoonist Peter
6 Fern leaf
7 Done without

8 Take a gander at
9 Soaked through
10 "__ Swell" (Rodgers & Hart song)
11 Big ape
12 Beer nickname
13 Chicago team
21 Nibbled (on)
23 Former
26 __ the Greek
28 Opera box
29 Cow calls
31 Chromosome description
32 Handy abbr.
36 Tropical fish
38 Modifies
39 War photographer Robert
40 First shepherd

41 Chime sound
43 Term of a show
46 Order a second printing of
49 Picks, as a major
51 Horse feet
52 Banks and Kovacs
53 Move a finger
56 Hebrew month
59 Forearm bone
61 Designer Ricci
62 Hoods' weapons
63 Play a role
64 It may be pitched
66 "We __ Family" (Sister Sledge tune)

CROSS-WORD PUZZLE

by Randolph Ross

ACROSS

1 Element #5
6 Bench pieces
11 Marked a ballot
14 Budget rival
15 Loggers' competition
16 Actress Charlotte
17 Baby Boomer successors
19 Genesis boat
20 Potter's need
21 Jamaican sectist
22 Computer magazine
23 Preceding night
25 Audience cries
27 Baby noodles
31 Nicholas Gage book
32 Sapporo sash
33 Lana Turner film
35 Observed
38 Milk-cap collectible
39 Med. test
40 Hard water?
41 William, to Charles
42 That certain something
46 You can dig it
47 Unfamiliar
49 Rejected
51 Bested
53 Red Zinger is one
54 Military insects
55 Boxer Griffith
59 Gangster's date
63 PTA interest
64 *Midnight Cowboy*, for one
66 Percent finish
67 Vertical number line
68 Like some gases
69 Gender
70 Pizzeria order
71 Claire of *Little Women*

DOWN

1 Luggage
2 Spread in a tub
3 Punjab princess
4 Brunch serving
5 Hide-hair connector
6 *Mlle.* of Madrid
7 Clark's coworker
8 Mucho
9 Readily explained
10 AL cap letters
11 Superman talent
12 Have an __ the ground
13 Fakes out a goalie
18 Ring or rink site
22 Proscribe
24 Vigor's partner
26 Reviewer Reed
27 Ice-cream creations
28 Peek finish
29 Document instruction
30 TV commercial maker
31 Issues forth
34 Parabolic path
36 Land unit
37 Unwanted plant
42 Noon, to Nero?
43 Part of FICA
44 Made a pick
45 Regret
48 Mormons: Abbr.
50 Loretta Young film of '36
51 Desert relief
52 "I give up!"
56 Long dress
57 Adjectival suffix
58 __ majesty
60 Hot spot
61 Turin cash, formerly
62 Allows
64 Some chromosomes
65 Ctr.

ACROSS

1 Colombian city
5 Fir variety
11 Elopers' helpers: Abbr.
14 Sharif or Bradley
15 Salad need
16 Wash. neighbor
17 Racing writer
19 With it
20 Skids
21 Repeal
22 Say "wheee!"
25 Soup grain
27 "That's __ excuse!" ("I don't buy it!")
28 Nautical spike
31 Class break
33 Placed carpet
34 EMT skill
37 Machine-gun sound
38 Optics prop
40 Exist
41 Ordinal ending
42 Paint badly
43 Arts supporter
46 Apathy
49 Succeeded as a siren
50 Sock pattern
52 Cashes in
54 Craze
55 Meanders
57 Former news initials
58 Ian Fleming's successor
63 Port storage spot
64 Twenty hundredweight
65 Competent
66 Paid notices
67 Relay-race props
68 Candied __

DOWN

1 *The Bride Came* __
2 Chartres chum
3 Body of *eau*
4 Vexatious
5 __ acid (antiseptic)
6 Garland
7 Designer wares
8 Assns.
9 Black bird
10 Short papers
11 George Smiley is one of his people
12 Joy's partner
13 1850s rebel
18 Takes wing
21 Samovar
22 __ aves
23 Vote for
24 *The Eagle Has Landed* author
25 Goodyear vehicle
26 Assist
29 Legal excuse
30 __ al-Khaimah (Arabian Gulf state)
32 Bowler's pickup
35 Introduction
36 Rips
39 Furrow
42 Actress Dolores __ Rio
44 Birch
45 *Mardi*, in Montana
47 Carrie or Louis
48 Zaragoza's province
50 Curaçao neighbor
51 Part of BART
53 Dame Edith
55 Hone
56 Word form for "within"
58 Exemplar of patience
59 "Coming in __ wing . . ."
60 Dr. J's org.
61 Shade tree
62 Where you live: Abbr.

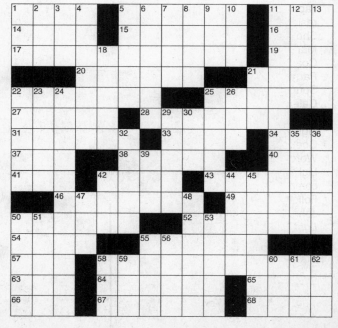

SEE 60 ACROSS

by Kenneth Lurye

ACROSS

1 Give it __ (take five)
6 It brought Hope to war zones
9 Word form for "wing"
14 "__ Thro' the Rye"
15 Swabbie's need
16 Went ballistic
17 Like a Brubeck tune's meter
19 Chemical compound
20 Remove
21 Eye drop
22 Eyeshade
23 Type of equation
26 Waylay
29 Certain Japanese resident
33 Showed again
34 Marine fossil
37 Coach Parseghian
38 Soup server
39 Calendar abbr.
40 Like most legislatures
43 Coeur d'__, ID
45 Word on an LP
46 Lighter-complected
47 Follower of John Biddle
51 *Lost Horizon* actress
54 "Unto us __ is given"
55 Singer Brickell
59 *Afternoon of __*
60 Theme of this puzzle
62 Instrumental effect
63 Wayfarer's stop
64 Muggy
65 *GMA* rival
66 Hall-of-Famer Williams
67 Some tourneys

DOWN

1 Obtained: Abbr.
2 Dissolute one
3 Actor Jannings
4 __ non (essential)
5 Explosive initials
6 Worked the plate
7 Word before wind or power
8 *Porgy and Bess*, e.g.
9 Restriction
10 Checker product
11 Auspices
12 Furnish anew
13 Swiss river
18 NBA team
24 Mil. branch
25 Painted metal
26 Some Middle Easterners
27 Deserve
28 Support
30 Baseball great Ralph
31 Make amends (for)
32 Defiant cry
34 Pavement material
35 Dietary data: Abbr.
36 Midwestern st.
38 Fifth-century Pope
41 Leafy vegetable
42 Stag
43 Car club
44 In a row
46 Huck or Mickey
48 Implied
49 Together
50 Drink order
51 Marshal Dillon
52 Hair style
53 Foray
56 Capitol topper
57 Victory cry
58 Remnants
61 Nevertheless, for short

by Gregory E. Paul

ACROSS

1 __ house (spy's retreat)
5 __ house (eatery)
9 Garden burrowers
14 Sub
15 Geometry calculation
16 Kicking's companion
17 War god
18 Dock
19 Crazy Horse's home
20 __ Tin Tin
21 City south of Provo
23 Dicta
25 Second sequel suffix
26 Auto part
27 Character for Camus or Heinlein
32 Western Starr
34 Akron products
35 Tokyo's old name
36 Gallic girlfriend
37 Marketing group
38 The Magi, e.g.
39 Pen brand
40 Applause
41 Sleigh puller
42 Bear State
44 "There once __ man . . ."
45 Toy ammo
46 White veggie
49 Arizona town
54 Golf-club part
55 Gave a hoot
56 Viva voce
57 Cap's partner
58 Quickly
59 Long ago
60 Goose relative
61 Dubbed
62 Elk, e.g.
63 Actress Sten

DOWN

1 Archaeologist's find
2 Home on high
3 Indiana town
4 Greek Aurora
5 Come to pass
6 Nobelist Oscar __ Sanchez
7 Caught, perhaps
8 Dutch spy
9 Olympic decathlete
10 Synthetic fiber
11 Chinese poet
12 Perpetually
13 Play a kids' game
21 Desiccated
22 Paddock parents
24 Playbill listing
27 Grain buildings
28 Vichy "very"
29 Philadelphia section
30 Adams or McClurg
31 46 Across, e.g.
32 Rum cake
33 Muslim prince
34 Exclamation of success
37 Author Sontag
38 Hurl
40 Prepared dough
41 Olds output
43 Per capita
44 "Honeysuckle Rose" writer
46 Follow the leader?
47 Herbert Hoover, for one
48 Neighbor of Del.
49 "__ See Clearly Now"
50 California wine valley
51 Apothecary's weight
52 Termite's meal
53 Seabird
57 Govt. purchasing org.

25 HOT STOVE LEAGUE

by Norma Steinberg

ACROSS

1 French-poodle name
5 Heidi's home
9 "Casey __ Bat"
14 Poems
15 Stock-exchange membership
16 Vocal ensemble
17 Toledo's capital
18 Preserve
19 Henna, e.g.
20 Description of Janus?
23 Mason's aide
24 Slalom
25 Bonkers
29 Thpeak like thith
31 Regal home
33 Deal in
36 Hall's partner
39 Fish eggs
40 Janitorial job?
44 Pie __ mode
45 *Norma* or *Carmen*
46 Rabbit __ (antenna)
47 Metal fasteners
49 Disney sci-fi film
52 Intuit
53 *"C'__ la vie!"*
56 Financially beset
60 Sale to a quilt maker?
63 __ grabs (available)
66 No-cholesterol spread
67 Run in neutral
68 Abolitionist author
69 Olfactory clue

70 "__ from New York, it's . . ."
71 Tortilla-chip dip
72 Ballpoints
73 Black and Red

DOWN

1 Goes under
2 Knucklehead
3 Thigh bone
4 Christopher's sponsor
5 Balance-sheet figure
6 Jacob's first wife
7 Uses macadam
8 Chuck, e.g.
9 Land measurement
10 All-you-can-eat portion

11 *Bon __* (fashionable)
12 "__ Eye Is on the Sparrow"
13 Before
21 Floral offering
22 Chops
26 Rooms in Pompeii
27 Stun
28 Adolescent years
30 Karol Wojtyla's title
32 "Do __ say, not . . ."
33 Muffler
34 J.R.'s mom
35 Take off
37 Loan info: Abbr.
38 Precisely

41 ". . . __ even a mouse"
42 Overturned
43 Vine parts
48 Nudges
50 Difficulties
51 Yoko __
54 Crouch
55 Spanish diacritical mark
57 Carrie's dad
58 Author __ Plain
59 Forest components
61 Vicinity
62 Lighting gas
63 Destroyer's monogram
64 Harper Valley org.
65 Coming next: Abbr.

by Dean Niles

ACROSS

1 Collect
6 Engine part, for short
10 West and Murray
14 Renaissance fiddle
15 Fragrance
16 To be, to Babette
17 Beatle surname
18 "__ Said" (Shirelles song)
19 Balsam or birch
20 Bret's TV brother
23 Greek T
26 Bonds
27 WWII vessels
28 Facet
30 *Antony and Cleopatra* role
31 *Knots Landing* star
34 '60s protest grp.
37 Baltic feeder
38 ". . . and __ sacred honor"
39 Portico
40 Tennis obstacle
41 Reds' ex-owner
45 __ *Dick*
46 Actress Mills
47 Booty
50 Pleased
52 Mess up
53 Seascape painter
56 Poker ritual
57 Back
58 Wanderer

62 "Like __ not!"
63 Road turn
64 Guy Williams role
65 Cloth surfaces
66 Jacuzzis
67 Flaming

DOWN

1 MGM motto start
2 Encountered
3 Attorneys' org.
4 Certain Slav
5 Where to start from
6 French title
7 __ apple
8 *"Arrivederci, __"*
9 Display of daring

10 Urban areas
11 Lighted courtyards
12 Upright
13 Tries to obtain
21 Comic Rudner
22 Abba of Israel
23 Toucan's toenail
24 In reserve
25 Tummy trouble
29 Attention
30 Hungarian leader Nagy
32 Actor Calhoun
33 Jerk
34 Mink piece
35 Indulgent one
36 Man-goat
39 Unforthcoming

41 Flanders of fiction
42 Soaks in
43 Counterfeit
44 Fancy musical flourish
45 Tightwads
47 Country lad
48 Historic ship
49 Winner's position
50 Gold Coast, today
51 Ladies' companions
54 Cry
55 Housetop
59 CAT scan cousin
60 Timetable abbr.
61 Female deer

27 THEY GOT LEGS

by Bob Lubbers

ACROSS

1 Toddler
4 Intoned
11 Harrison or Reed
14 Gershwin brother
15 Change the form of
16 First lady
17 *Rhoda* mother
19 Ate
20 Earthquake __ (Dogpatch tough)
21 Really weird
23 Marty or Steve
24 Sashes
26 Flowing rock
29 Requirement
30 Give __ for one's money
31 Exhausted
32 General Bradley
33 Prejudiced
34 Gravel-voiced actor
38 Broncos' turf
39 Ripped
40 Come in
41 French city
42 "Phooey!"
46 Kick
47 Trail shelter
48 Briquette rack
49 Turkish bigwig
51 Singer Yearwood
52 Every one
54 Hollywood columnist
57 Yellow or Black
58 Abrasives
59 WSW opposite
60 Islet
61 Strips
62 June honoree

DOWN

1 Jack Haley role
2 Seer of a sort
3 Hair trouble
4 Have a shoulder to __
5 Felled by an ax
6 Simile center
7 Lemieux's league
8 Alter, perhaps
9 Fencing swords
10 Author Earl __ Biggers
11 Practice
12 Actress Le Gallienne
13 Marked a ballot
18 Like some dorms
22 Homeric epic
24 Kind of exam
25 *Resurrection* actress
27 Swerve
28 Sum (up)
30 Part of USA
31 Fork prong
32 Singular person
33 Silo neighbor
34 Carson replacer
35 Bring __ (make use of)
36 __ Culp Hobby
37 Honk
38 Society newcomer
41 Heavy
42 Faucet fault
43 Grated
44 Goddess of wisdom
45 Wept
47 Central idea
48 Icky
50 Drop fur
51 *Of __ I Sing*
52 Inquire
53 Golf star Trevino
55 *Red River* actress
56 Assist

by Dean Niles

ACROSS

1 "Deck the Halls" finish
5 Cambodian language
10 Saintly image
14 Baseballer Felipe
15 Savoir-__
16 __ contendere
17 Wasserstein play, with *The*
20 Varnish ingredient
21 Alienate
22 Auto pioneer
25 Reaction to a rat
26 Ernie Els' grp.
29 Field
31 Queue after Q
36 Hasty flight
37 Interlace
39 Smash ending
40 Hansberry play
44 *Leave __ Me*
45 *Parade* composer
46 Play a part
47 Stuff
50 Dickens character
51 Questioning grunts
52 Cross letters
54 Stagger
56 Bibliophile's holder
61 Used the microwave
65 Kushner play
68 Jazz guitarist Charlie
69 __ of the trade
70 Heavy metal
71 Former spouses
72 Kicks in
73 Actress Merrill

DOWN

1 Cowardly Lion portrayer
2 Nautical adverb
3 Hi's wife
4 Sound portion
5 Fast-food co.
6 Hoo-__ (to-do)
7 Swampy land
8 Uneven
9 Tenant
10 Old Peruvian
11 City in *Deutschland*
12 Designer Cassini
13 It can really smell
18 Acquired family
19 Annoys
23 *Zwei* follower
24 Connery and O'Casey
26 Braid hair
27 Singer Brooks
28 Stradivari's teacher
30 For the birds
32 Golf peg
33 Bears: Lat.
34 Certify, with "for"
35 Inclinations
38 Computer key
41 Charged atom
42 Mah-jongg piece
43 Author Hanff
48 "The __ From Ipanema"
49 California peak
53 Offspring
55 Like pulp fiction
56 Ruth's nickname
57 Figurine mineral
58 Storybook villain
59 Some gym shoes
60 Chignon
62 __ Te Kanawa
63 A social sci.
64 Actress Delany
66 Frothy brew
67 Bks. in progress

by Eileen Lexau

ACROSS

1 __ steer (bad advice)
4 Word of praise
8 Tend the turkey
13 Cartoonist Peter
14 Actress Raines
15 Tailor
16 Kind of deed
18 Scandinavian toast
19 *Wait __ Dark*
20 Sports no-no
22 Cathedral feature
23 Went to Wendy's
25 Chicken, in Chihuahua
27 __-foot oil
30 Far-out person
33 *Time* founder Henry
36 No-good
38 Morse unit
39 Newspaper page
40 Sot
41 Fast time
42 One __ time
43 Spanish bread
44 Therefore
45 Tile artwork
47 Moisten again
49 Candice's dad
51 Fabric sample
55 Bean curd
57 Most August babies
60 Jetson kid
61 Old Roman official
63 Football play
65 Categorizes
66 Sweetie
67 Get close to
68 Hank of hair
69 Chatters
70 Sea bird

DOWN

1 Main impact
2 Get together
3 Made a gesture
4 Toothpaste type
5 Patron saint of Scandinavia
6 Hodgepodge
7 Keep pent
8 __-relief
9 Acid neutralizer
10 Instruction to a broker
11 Afternoon parties
12 Agatha contemporary
13 Bluish green
17 Board game
21 Nonintellectuals
24 Battlefront adjective
26 Rocket expert Willy
28 Disney sci-fi film
29 Fantastic
31 Small dent
32 Comic-strip dog
33 Soil of a sort
34 Capable of
35 Truce
37 Insignificant
41 Not to mention
43 Understand
46 Grownups
48 Vase-shaped jug
50 Oboelike
52 More faithful
53 Role for Arnold
54 Word form for "water"
55 Trial
56 Reputation
58 __-Day vitamins
59 Minn. neighbor
62 Curve shape
64 Part of MGM's motto

by Randolph Ross

ACROSS

1 Gyro ingredient
5 __ acid
10 Dangerous snakes
14 Concert halls
15 Baseball great Paul
16 Bernard, once of CNN
17 Party pooper
19 Mexican moolah
20 Terns and erns
21 Regarding this point
23 Tramp's mate
24 Gentle hit
25 Poe family
28 Cash in
29 Standard and __
30 Rock drummer Helm
31 Good times
34 Makes lace
35 Do studio work
36 Cruising
37 Signs off on
38 He played Wyatt and Eliot
39 Sardonic look
40 Ready the VCR
42 Fills the shelves
43 Poem part
45 Llama land
46 Nixon daughter
47 Windfalls
51 Standing
52 Spousal secrets
54 Advantage
55 Kuwaiti royal
56 Quaker pronoun
57 Adam or Rebecca
58 Rider's prods
59 Fairy-tale opener

DOWN

1 Financial-page info
2 "Zip-__-Doo-Dah"
3 Prefix for physics
4 Nonsense spouters
5 Tony and Edgar
6 Actor Patinkin
7 Signs
8 Maiden-name indicator
9 Conforming to a doctrine
10 On __ (binging)
11 Note paper?
12 Trattoria selection
13 Eagle's maneuver
18 Tale tellers
22 Balanced
24 *Sliver* author
25 Until
26 Drench
27 Arkansas resort
28 Pay the bill
30 Flood preventer
32 Fringe benefit
33 5th Avenue store
35 Molds differently
36 Become
38 De Gaulle's cap
39 Proverbial back breaker
41 Pyrotechnic device
42 Men of La Mancha
43 Spread
44 Exchange
45 Gondola worker
47 Cordon __
48 Newswoman Paula
49 Pianist Templeton
50 __-ball (arcade game)
53 Troublesome tyke

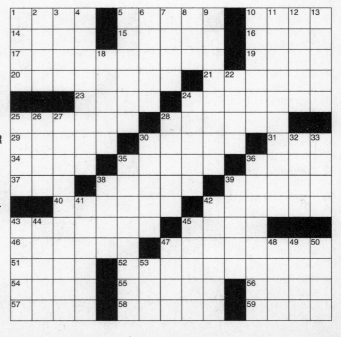

31 GRIDDLE-ISMS

by Bob Lubbers

ACROSS

1 Deprivation
5 Bagel relative
10 Droops
14 Buck ending
15 *Rocky IV* villain
16 Capri, e.g.
17 Hedge
20 Candidate list
21 Raw, as copy
22 Corn spikes
25 Twosome
26 Make a drop-flat landing
32 __ Faithful
33 Obey
34 1 to 10, for one
36 "Now __ this!"
38 Hogwash
41 Govt. agent
42 Craze
44 Binge
46 JFK posting
47 Honor, as a best man
51 Take to court
52 Judge Roy __
53 Aches and pains
58 Cable network
62 Dawdle
65 "So be it"
66 __ trip (travel)
67 Give off
68 Gun-sight segments
69 Willow twig
70 Derides

DOWN

1 Senate concerns
2 Kind of hygiene
3 Couch
4 Butter up
5 Ike's monogram
6 Spanish gold
7 Mork utterance
8 East African state
9 Work the muscles
10 Juan's emphatic agreement
11 CEO's aide
12 Stickum
13 Begonia-to-be
18 Expert on the rich and famous
19 Role models
23 Charlotte's kin
24 Slant
26 Dress fold
27 Bell town
28 Mrs. Bunker
29 Behave
30 Identified
31 Gladden
32 Resistance unit
35 Disney deer
37 Inlet
39 Leopold's partner
40 Stud site
43 Resource
45 Comics cop
48 Find, as a radio signal
49 Aquarium fish
50 Foot part
53 At a distance
54 *My Friend* __
55 Fibbed
56 Rockies, e.g.: Abbr.
57 Short-story author
59 Western Indian
60 Expatriate of 8 Down
61 Profits
63 Tiny
64 Swiss river

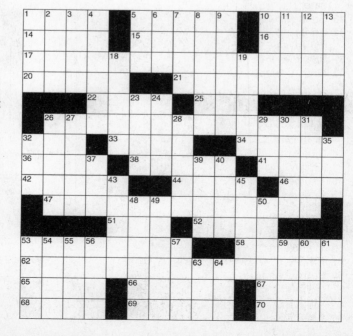

ACROSS

1 Strongman Charles
6 Fourposters
10 Oversize hairdo
14 Destroy
15 Make changes to
16 Songbird
17 Bay city
18 Minuscule
19 Fontanne's partner
20 STRIKE
23 Skater Midori
24 Padre, for short
25 Most loyal
27 European region
30 Broadway eatery
33 Caesar's 401
34 Canadian native
37 Scandinavian
38 Math. subject
39 WHACK
41 Under the weather
42 Varnish ingredient
44 Director Kazan
45 Teachers' org.
46 Believes in
48 CD units
51 Beats badly
54 Wire measure
55 Tie holder
57 PINCH
62 Bauxite and galena
64 Entreaty
65 Pluralizers
66 Get up
67 Aromatic veggie
68 Devise a new plat
69 *Atlantis* group
70 Spanish compass point
71 Sports data

DOWN

1 One of the Aleutians
2 Mine car
3 Light source
4 Hope for, with "to"
5 Generous one
6 Casino activity
7 Decree
8 Bahrain money
9 Cutting tool
10 Hole maker
11 PUNCH
12 *La Bohème*, updated
13 Not fooled by
21 Put out
22 Stood (against)
26 Theater notice: Abbr.
27 Lazybones
28 HIT
29 Commedia dell'__
31 The Bahamas, e.g.
32 Actress Ward
33 Market wagon
35 Moray
36 Send forth
39 Pot starters
40 Ohio city
43 Haifa's loc.
47 Demo
49 Target seekers
50 Clothes holder
52 Bucks and toms
53 Winter hazard
55 Having divided loyalties
56 Diva's specialty
58 Trout source
59 U.S. Grant's alma mater
60 Orderly
61 Baking amts.
63 Vast amount

33 PICTURE THIS

by Jim Page

ACROSS

1 Knife handles
6 Ark passenger
10 Culture medium
14 Bee-related
15 Musical motif
16 Pianist Peter
17 '70s nightspot
18 Canter control
19 Melee
20 Versatile one
23 Hit with a ray gun
24 Royal caretaker
25 Ghostly toon
29 Great __ (Bahamian island)
31 German river
32 Arizona river
34 Superior
38 *Magic Flute* character
41 Word with sixth or common
42 Type assortment
43 Trig term
44 Collar holders
46 Enthusiastic about
48 Little swine
51 It's on the edge
52 Ruler of nursery songs
59 Fused: Fr.
60 Part of UAR
61 Ibis' cousin
62 Greek conflict
63 Container allowance
64 Fix
65 Mailed away
66 *Cleopatra*, for one
67 Reeboks alternatives

DOWN

1 Trip to Mecca
2 Samoan port
3 Royal treasury
4 Board nail
5 Grab some Z's
6 Thong
7 Bread endpiece
8 Olympian Zátopek
9 Hindu incantation
10 Adversary
11 Decorative stone
12 Lauder competitor
13 Perch
21 Wells' partner
22 Scout about, for short
25 French roosters
26 Together: Mus.
27 Called, at poker
28 Media contact
29 Marian Anderson et al.
30 German road
33 Not definite
35 Week-ending initials
36 "This can't be!"
37 Word form for "wing"
39 Tidy: It.
40 Set of values
45 __ would have it (by chance)
47 Certain Midwesterner
48 Gull-like birds
49 Turning point
50 Salad ingredient
51 Fiddle precursor
53 Skeet's starting point
54 Last name in espionage
55 Sweet beginning
56 Arduous journey
57 Solitary
58 Winds up

34 FOR THE BIRDS

by Fred Piscop

ACROSS

1 Wall Street figure
7 Meat in a can
11 Auto part
14 February plea
15 Narrow way
16 "I __ Rock"
17 Cures meat
18 Relievers' stats
19 Took the gold
20 Avian markers?
22 Blended
23 Beard
24 Sports legend Zaharias
25 Aah's partner
28 Decade parts: Abbr.
29 *Flash Gordon*, e.g.
31 Half a train?
33 __ around (gridiron play)
35 Binge
36 *Car 54* character
38 Drawer or shelf preceder
40 Nasty
43 Tailless amphibian
45 Angular lead-in
47 Was aware of
48 Victor of filmdom
50 Well contents
52 "Wow!"
53 Evangelist Roberts
54 Lorraine of *GoodFellas*
57 *Platoon* setting
58 Avian snack food?
63 Author Levin
64 Annapolis sch.
65 *Breathless* actor
66 __ Tech
67 Egyptian goddess
68 Hospital solution
69 Munched on
70 Actress Daly
71 Intertwine

DOWN

1 1/2 fl. oz.
2 San __, Italy
3 One way to run
4 Dam kin
5 Zing
6 Evaluate anew
7 Winter forecast
8 "Gay" city
9 Three-syllable foot
10 Boot-camp chow
11 Avian phone feature?
12 Pond denizen
13 Howie of *St. Elsewhere*
21 Lacks
24 Jack Palance series of '75
25 Columbus Day mo.
26 Taunting cry
27 Avian spicy dish?
30 Dawn goddess
32 Hall of Famer Lefty
34 Tiny circle
37 Agile
39 Thorn mishap
41 Poor grade
42 Ram's dam
44 *La Mer* composer
46 Tick off
48 Steffi rival
49 Biblical mount
51 Person from Pusan
55 Arrested
56 __ of mistaken identity
58 Knock it off
59 Crystallize
60 __ Minor
61 Not diluted: Abbr.
62 Wounded __, SD

35 TIED UP

by Rich Norris

ACROSS

1 Family member
4 Bribable
9 IOU
13 Once again
15 Appliance name
16 Wine: Pref.
17 Sound producers
19 Extreme anger
20 Plea
21 Swapped
23 Notwithstanding
24 Foppish one
25 Mellow, maybe
26 Hit the mall
27 Little rascal
30 Last inning, usually
33 Docks
34 Actress Peeples
35 Words of dread
36 Filled
37 Abe's coin
38 Prosecutors: Abbr.
39 Incurred, as a bill
40 "Wake Up, Little __"
41 GA summer setting
42 Is in debt
43 Rocky peak
44 Lineage
46 Kander/Ebb musical
50 Drunk
52 One of these days
53 Breathe heavily
54 In trouble
56 Jason's ship
57 Kilmer poem
58 Flat fee
59 Coarse file
60 "He __ got a clue!"
61 Byways: Abbr.

DOWN

1 Held onto
2 "__ ear and out . . ."
3 Religious groups
4 Leave the premises
5 Ham it up
6 Not any
7 Also
8 Arguer's desire
9 Reef material
10 Column toppers
11 *Picnic* playwright
12 Word after open or pigeon
14 On the __ (angry)
18 Actress Jennifer Jason
22 Account execs
24 Docile ones
26 Legal locale
28 Skirt length
29 Appetizer choice
30 Stocking shade
31 "If __ a Hammer"
32 Richard Rodgers musical
33 Window sections
36 Part of a serrated edge
37 Museum worker
39 Chess piece
40 Solemn
43 Least wild
45 Winning
46 Comic Myron
47 Not as green
48 Fix
49 Tries out
50 Warm up with Tyson
51 Scarlett's home
52 Fr. holy women
55 Powerful DC lobby

by Patrick Jordan

ACROSS

1 Lucie's dad
5 Water-balloon sound
10 Keep __ (persist)
14 Part of QED
15 Singer Abdul
16 Flicka, e.g.
17 Mae West
19 School grps.
20 Stoical type
21 Carries through
23 Octopus defenses
25 List of names
26 Wood-shaping tool
28 Nightmarish street
31 Minds
34 Plant a bug
35 "Don't move!"
37 Bathwater tester
38 John Hancock
41 Actress Hagen
42 Went a-wandering
43 Brown brews
44 Baseball star Puckett
46 MGM mascot
47 Cal. abbr.
48 Ticks off
50 Say "Yay" at Shea
52 Giving freely
56 Couplings
60 Fancy
61 Annie Oakley
63 Foreman's weapon
64 Banded gemstone
65 Neighborhood
66 Hart's former ET cohost
67 Mazatlán mister
68 Godiva, for one

DOWN

1 Salami shop
2 Clapton or Idle
3 Not out
4 Lists deductions
5 Punish, perhaps
6 Lobbying grp.
7 Biblical physician
8 Swoosie, on *Sisters*
9 Colloquial tuber
10 Medicine vial
11 Playground fink
12 *Dies* follower
13 Hardy girl
18 Tarzan's mate
22 Songwriter Leonard
24 Soap, e.g.
26 "__ a stinker?": Bugs Bunny
27 Dismal state
29 "__ Entertain You"
30 Shower component
32 Taj Mahal features
33 Meets, as a bet
34 *The Winds of War* novelist
35 Back
36 Londoner's last letter
39 More ironic
40 Seafaring
45 Puff of wind
47 Author Morrison
49 Living-room items
51 *The __ Limits*
52 Present
53 Adams or McClurg
54 Egg on
55 Playwright O'Casey
57 Gumbo green
58 Requirement
59 Collar rib
62 Ike's WWII command

37 TEN HUT!

by Gregory E. Paul

ACROSS

1 Diving duck
5 James __ Garfield
10 Eating plan
14 Vagabond
15 Blackmore heroine
16 Fairy-tale opener
17 Daredevil Knievel
18 Actor Davis
19 To be, to Satie
20 Bush conveyance
23 Work smoothly
24 Eye part
25 Cubbyhole
27 Clearheaded
30 Safari sights
33 Trig, e.g.
36 Hideout
38 Soprano Lucine
39 "__ du lieber!"
40 Mansion worker
42 Family vehicle
43 Singer Bonnie
45 *Nautilus* man
46 Computer unit
47 Eastwood costar of '95
49 Postpone
51 Coped (with)
53 Feudal vassals
57 Evian, e.g.
59 Devil dogs' tune
62 Dumbbell move
64 Sinful city
65 *My Friend* __
66 Shells and such
67 Garry or Dudley
68 Swerve
69 2-time NL MVP
70 ". . . man, __, a canal . . ."
71 Villa d'__

DOWN

1 Harvest wool
2 In-flight entertainment
3 1975 Pulitzer winner
4 Rapacious
5 Cute
6 Pear variety
7 Bouquet favorite
8 Charged atom
9 Eenie follower
10 Female goat
11 Village People song
12 Beige
13 Abound
21 Lennon's lady
22 Showy display
26 Easter dish
28 Deserve
29 Rosie's pin
31 "Confound it!"
32 Levelheaded
33 Hershey rival
34 One-__ (ball game)
35 Patton's command
37 "__ Lama Ding Dong"
40 Power source
41 Blue bloods
44 Golf gizmo
46 High hairdo
48 Blood fluid
50 Fleur-de-__
52 Cavalry unit
54 Circles
55 Ant
56 Trap
57 Con game
58 Cougar
60 Graven image
61 Director Ephron
63 Part of UCLA

by Chuck Deodene

ACROSS

1 Platter
5 Certain Peruvian
10 *Rent-__* (Reynolds film)
14 Funny bone neighbor
15 Minnesota city
16 Govern
17 Concert ender
18 Defensive lineman
20 Of an eye part
22 Discharge
23 Drum site
24 Vietnamese waterway
28 Yale students
29 Last Supper setting
33 Pendant
36 Sprat's diet
38 Film __
39 Narc's pooch
44 "La __ Bonita" (Madonna tune)
45 Comic Jay
46 "It's __-win situation!"
47 University unit
51 Entr'__
53 New Age treatment
58 Flabbergast
61 Horned vipers
62 Country-music guitar
63 1980 J. Geils Band song
67 Swiped
68 Kinnear of *Sabrina*
69 Spinning about
70 Mothballed
71 Nautical prefix
72 Ferraro's nickname
73 Clamp shapes

DOWN

1 Found via research
2 __ *Lucy*
3 Condescending expression
4 Burgundy vessel
5 Actor Cariou
6 Nuptial phrase
7 Tightwad
8 Lacking pep
9 Inhabitant
10 Curved path
11 Salad slice, for short
12 Stewpot
13 Social equal
19 ". . . a __ o'clock scholar"
21 Respites
25 Demeanor
26 *La Bamba* actor Morales
27 Used the phone
30 Sonata ending
31 Androcles' friend
32 Thus
33 Depositor's protector: Abbr.
34 ". . . __ I've been told"
35 Pamplona hazard
37 Tagliabue's org.
40 Wingding
41 Accomplishment
42 Ruler marking
43 Renowned
48 Geological periods
49 Attend without a date
50 Domain
52 Like Henry Miller's novels
54 Seven-Emmy winner
55 Habitation
56 Wage earner, in Britain
57 Ox collars
58 Marine life
59 Was clad in
60 At any time
64 Self-esteem
65 Plunk or flooey lead-in
66 Crafty

39 GROUPIES

by Gregory E. Paul

ACROSS

1 Charles' princedom
6 Two together
10 Can. province
14 Separated
15 Nautical adverb
16 Richard of *A Summer Place*
17 Air sign
18 Actress Patricia
19 __ it (amen)
20 Papal name
21 Top-rank
24 Loverboy
26 Opal, e.g.
27 Slat
29 Play thing
34 *Roots* Emmy winner
35 *Les __-Unis*
36 Dander
37 Recipe verb
38 Designer Simpson
39 Word on a penny
40 Racer Fabi
41 Perfect person
42 Novelist Puzo
43 Chanteur
45 Desolate
46 Whopper
47 Tropical fish
48 CNN round table, with *The*
53 Naval noncom
56 Wilma's hubby
57 Shade of blue
58 Scarlett's mother
60 Monster
61 Monstrous
62 Newsboy's concern
63 Mean-spirited
64 Upset
65 Serious

DOWN

1 Stock-exchange street
2 Cap-__ (head to toe)
3 American Federation of Teachers, e.g.
4 Be human
5 Speak hesitatingly
6 "Dueling" instrument
7 Butterine
8 Wear's partner
9 New York City waterway
10 Ali Baba word
11 Spellbound
12 The Elephant Boy
13 Place for a pad
22 Atmospheric word form
23 Diagnostic tests, for short
25 Walkie-talkie word
27 Shoe forms
28 Path starter
29 Guide the ride
30 Like some tales
31 Environmental group
32 "Mr. Cub" Banks
33 River in Montana
35 Precipice
38 UC-Irvine student
39 Dray
41 __ were (so to speak)
42 Crèche items
44 Porch swing
45 Outlaw
47 *Atlantic City* director
48 Corp. VIPs
49 Southern constellation
50 Llama land
51 Jeans name
52 Inventor Borden
54 Senator Domenici
55 Beaut
59 Card game

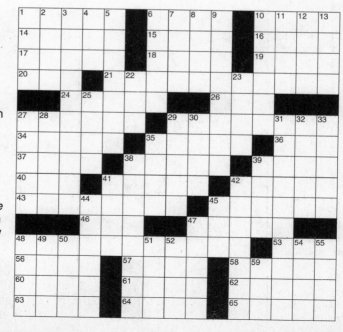

40 SNOOPY BRITS

by Dean Niles

ACROSS

1 Embark on a tirade
5 *The Seven Year Itch* star
10 Despot
14 Baseball manager Felipe
15 *West Side Story* role
16 Nevada city
17 Linseed-oil source
18 Computer command
19 Vocal range
20 Doyle snoop
23 The Belmonts' lead singer
24 Leavening
25 Long awning
28 HBO medium
31 "Farewell!"
32 Wood wedge
33 "__ bodkins!"
36 Sayers snoop
40 Word form for "equal"
41 Springiness
42 Taj __
43 Key material
45 Bogie costar
46 Orange Bowl locale
49 Flowing robe
50 Dexter snoop
56 Wine valley
57 Biblical mount
58 Muck or mire
60 Unique fellow
61 Where the action is
62 Film genre
63 Tenant's requirement
64 Clarabell colleague
65 Cognizant of

DOWN

1 UK fleet
2 "__ fair in love . . ."
3 Big name in lexicography
4 In black tie
5 Take on
6 LBJ's __ Poverty
7 Leif's dad
8 Unite
9 Wood strip
10 County Kerry seat
11 Alabama city
12 Contributes
13 Perch
21 Shred
22 Olive of comics
25 Colombian city
26 Fusses
27 Robert De __
28 Chase the comic
29 Million suffix
30 Upscale wheels
32 Rile
33 Workplace agcy.
34 "It's agreed!"
35 Word part: Abbr.
37 I: Lat.
38 Adult insect
39 Word in "Yankee Doodle"
43 Bestow
44 Contend
45 Indian port
46 Unimportant
47 Ludicrous
48 Trembling poplar
49 General course
51 African nation
52 Lawn-mower brand
53 Layered cookie
54 Any day now
55 Basso Pinza
59 Sea bird

41 ANIMAL ACTS

by Mark Diehl

ACROSS

1 Branch
5 ". . . __ man with seven wives"
10 Baloney
14 Draft rating
15 Southern accent
16 Choir member
17 Ballroom dance
19 *Dr. Zhivago* director
20 An archangel
21 Farewell appearance
23 Ignites
26 Solo performance
27 Actor Calhoun
29 Mennonite sect
33 Double curve
36 Taos tie
37 Eaves dropper
38 '60s dance
41 Built __ (durable)
42 Actor Arkin
43 Gridiron stats: Abbr.
44 Off the cuff
45 Czech, for one
46 Source
48 Gets together (with)
54 Novelty dance
58 Muskie's state
59 Buffalo's water
60 Soldier's strides
63 Turns brown
64 One with big eyes
65 Single apartment
66 Rathskeller offerings
67 "__ Dawn" (Reddy song)
68 Hand, across the border

DOWN

1 Yoga position
2 Adapt (to)
3 Raise reason
4 Makes cakes
5 Charley Weaver's Mount __
6 *The A-Team* star
7 Corn units
8 Like Dick Tracy's wrist radio
9 Place of worship
10 Vinegar variety
11 Bread spread
12 Mr. Musial
13 __ Kong
18 "Evil Woman" band, for short
22 A B vitamin
24 Weather system
25 Music genre
28 Blue-blooded
30 Distasteful
31 *Citizen Kane* prop
32 Some turkeys
33 Sundance's girl
34 Wearing loafers
35 Bearish order
36 Cafeteria worker
37 "__ a dream": King
39 Impartiality
40 *B.C.* buck
45 Moe or Larry
47 George Burns film
49 Els' followers
50 Ryan's daughter
51 Tuscany town
52 Let one's hair down, perhaps
53 Pasta sauce
54 VHS alternative
55 River to the Caspian Sea
56 75% of a dozen
57 Harris undertaking
61 Salon job
62 Time period

SOLITARY SOLVING

by Patrick Jordan

ACROSS

1 Give off vapors
5 Fate
10 Lie next to
14 Orwell's alma mater
15 Regular order
16 Welles role
17 Mickey's maker
18 Martini partner
19 Netman Nastase
20 "I'm Into Something Good" band
23 Feel off
24 Bump on a log
25 Alleged Garbo comment
33 Cadre
34 Malicious
35 Addl. phone
37 Pâté de __ gras
38 Dayan of Israel
39 Knight's club
40 "You bet!"
41 Curry component
42 Like Cheerios
43 TV tuners
46 Nabokov novel
47 Electrical unit
48 *Quiz Show* locale
56 PBS series
57 Non-studio film, for short
58 Hoop star O'Neal, in headlines
60 African republic
61 *The Way __ Flesh*
62 Icicle base
63 Sanctified
64 "The Highwayman" poet
65 At love, perhaps

DOWN

1 Hardly any
2 Promontory Point state
3 Double agent
4 Infatuate
5 Network newsman Charles
6 ". . . unto us __ is born"
7 Bandleader Columbo
8 Livestock feed
9 Make an enemy of
10 With hands on hips
11 Java neighbor
12 College course section
13 Kicker's props
21 Tiny bit
22 Manageable
25 Questionable
26 He comes a-courtin'
27 Join the rebellion
28 "__, All Ye Faithful"
29 __ *Instinct*
30 Cultural prefix
31 "Peachy keen!"
32 Distinguish oneself
36 Addition column
38 Sci-fi phenomenon
39 Small monkey
41 Fugue ending
42 Roman emperor
44 Affliction
45 Annual prizes
48 Move a little
49 London area
50 Racetrack shape
51 Data
52 Singer Anita
53 Khartoum's river
54 Bangkok citizen
55 Dine on
59 Proof abbr.

43 SLEEPY TOWNS

by Bob Lubbers

ACROSS

1 Sups
6 "__ girl!"
10 Flu shots, e.g.
14 Astaire's sister
15 Canadian bird
16 Oklahoma city
17 __, MA
19 OTB postings
20 Party pro
21 Give out
23 Ike's command: Abbr.
24 Ooze
26 Antipasto items
29 __ Xiaoping
31 Library tool
34 Big barrel
35 Conger
38 Tardy
40 __, ME
43 Immense
44 Collector's goal
45 Seine sight
46 Film award
48 Con game
52 __ on Sunday
54 City on the Wailuku
57 Airline to Tokyo
58 Proficient
61 Graduate course
63 Against
65 __, NJ
67 Swag
68 Netman Nastase
69 Non-studio movie, for short
70 Flubs
71 Guide
72 Position

DOWN

1 Cakewalked
2 Conceive
3 Wayne or Isaac
4 Dresden river
5 Crystal-ball gazers
6 Lord Tennyson
7 Also
8 Spelling the actress
9 "No ifs, __, or buts!"
10 Korean capital
11 Exert oneself
12 Disencumber
13 TV spots
18 Actress Ruby
22 Abrasion
25 __, KY
27 Trading center
28 Pigpen
30 Actress Rowlands
32 Can material
33 Wapitis
36 Audience demand
37 Allows
39 Young 'uns
40 Cabbage kin
41 One way up
42 Paper Mate rival
43 Rummy game
47 Chanced
49 Alberta's home
50 Bayer rival
51 Identified
53 Oversees copy
55 General at Gettysburg
56 All: Lat.
59 *Murphy Brown* barkeep
60 Fib
62 Lacks existence
63 Pub serving
64 Negative connector
66 OSS successor

44 IT'S ACADEMIC

by Gerald R. Ferguson

ACROSS

1 Diamond corner
5 Newsman Huntley
9 Lawful volunteers
14 Unsuitable for farming
15 Sci-fi award
16 Hippodrome
17 Students' sports grp.
18 "Rush it" letters
19 Nobelist Pauling
20 Generally accepted facts
23 Ottoman ruler
24 Egg layer
25 Lacey's partner
29 Lookouts, e.g.
34 Arch types
35 Abner's adjective
36 Nanki-__
37 Disputed point
42 Took the bait
43 Black cuckoo
44 Actress Mills
45 Winter hiking need
48 Vocation
49 "Adam and Eve __ raft!"
50 Cry of surprise
51 Ideological belief
60 Painter Veronese
61 Choir member
62 Jocularity
63 Castaway's spot
64 Pro-shop buy
65 Byron poem
66 Wee
67 Mary or Gary
68 Midmonth day

DOWN

1 French bench
2 Exxon rival
3 Famous twins' home
4 Wax-covered cheese
5 Quasimodo portrayer
6 Dog of the Yukon
7 Former Alaska governor
8 "__ the morning!"
9 Warehouse platform
10 Direct (toward)
11 __ packing (evict)
12 Comfy
13 Slacken
21 Very heavy
22 Pup
25 Searches thoroughly
26 Once more
27 Reach
28 Hoop skirt?
29 Caine role
30 Thumbnail sketch
31 Express oneself
32 Arledge of ABC
33 Naval acronym
38 1992 Indy winner
39 Beatle bride
40 Pocatello's state
41 Hide-hair connector
46 Bulky cloth
47 Snobbish
48 Show partner
50 Weasel relative
51 __ and polish
52 Docket entry
53 Mender's target
54 Courtroom ritual
55 Word before collar or market
56 Wrinkled fruit
57 Hefty rival
58 At this place
59 Afternoon receptions

45 LITTERARY

by Dean Niles

ACROSS

1 Chanteuse Edith
5 Life, in La Paz
9 Large parrot
14 Word form for "height"
15 Culture medium
16 Mistreatment
17 First infatuation
19 Wearing a toga
20 Word on Irish coins
21 Spills the beans, with "out"
22 Monopoly props
26 7-Up rival
28 Took a breath
30 __ Tin Tin
31 Scoreboard nos.
34 Marks to retain
35 Rubber gasket
37 Sound of discovery
38 Kin
39 Didn't move
40 Chicago paper, for short
41 Grounded bird
42 __-France
43 Learner
44 Reading room
45 It may be the word
46 Part of some acts
48 Pants protector
51 Rue
52 Regardless
54 Give __ for one's money
56 Irish dramatist Brendan
57 Wright place at the right time
62 Bring forth
63 With: Fr.
64 Parrot or ape
65 Boutonniere site
66 Hart's ex-cohost
67 "Cool it!"

DOWN

1 Baby food
2 *ER* location
3 Dadaist Hans
4 Dandy
5 Luggage piece
6 Marty Feldman role
7 Barry and Brubeck
8 *You __ There*
9 Fertilizing, in a way
10 *All __ Eve*
11 Jimmy Olsen, e.g.
12 "I'd hate to break up __"
13 Brings together
18 Rebel cries
21 Seawater
22 Greeted the villain
23 Promptly
24 1952 Ray Anthony tune
25 Gobbles up
27 Holds dear
29 Money
32 Filch
33 "Amen!"
36 Serling or Steiger
39 Changeable
40 __ oil (varnish agent)
42 Seat the jury
43 Really small
47 Forked support
49 Conscious
50 Ingenuous
52 First second son
53 Leningrad river
55 Hwys.
57 *Krazy __*
58 "__ a Rebel"
59 Go through the motions
60 One of the 5 W's
61 Keystone officer

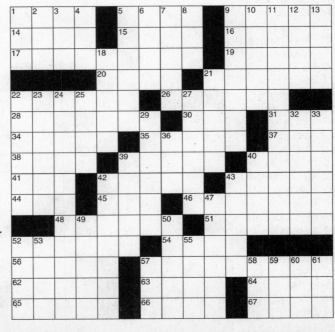

MOVIE MISTERS

by Gregory E. Paul

ACROSS

1 Weather systems
5 Pair of mules
9 Like Batman
14 "Uh-huh"
15 Windex target
16 Fred's sister
17 Writer Waugh
18 Not fooled by
19 Flower feature
20 Mr. Chips
23 Compass pt.
24 Poet Thomas
25 Talk show pioneer
27 City on the Willamette
30 Meara's partner
33 Genetic abbr.
34 Rival of Coco
37 Rope loop
38 Broadcasts
40 *The Crucible* locale
42 56 Down designer
43 Panache
45 Gold weight
47 Clergyman: Abbr.
48 Jailbreaker
50 Poser's word
52 Mayberry lad
53 Son of Jacob
55 Fuss
57 Mr. Belvedere
62 Red Cloud's residence
64 Traipse
65 Birth of a notion
66 Marlin's milieu
67 Baseballer Manny
68 Actress Naldi
69 Malory's *Le __ d'Arthur*
70 ". . . __ o'clock scholar"
71 Make tight

DOWN

1 Dissembler
2 European capital
3 Football coach Ewbank
4 Withdraw
5 Squeaky-clean
6 World Wildlife Fund symbol
7 Dramatist Chekhov
8 Sign gas
9 Queeg, for one
10 Summer drink
11 Mr. Moto
12 Zest
13 Editor's marking
21 Sandberg of baseball
22 Likely
26 Succulent plant
27 Clear the board
28 Army outfits
29 Mr. Deeds
30 Nostradamus, e.g.
31 Adlai's running mate
32 Town officer
35 Seize
36 Old scale note
39 Open-hand blow
41 Village People song
44 Unisex
46 "And next . . ."
49 Sniggler's catch
51 Rommel et al.
53 Going on
54 Opine
55 Bohr's bit
56 Art __
58 Cookbook author Rombauer
59 Singer Adams
60 Key letter
61 False god
63 Munch

47 MAKE-UP TEST

by Norma Steinberg

ACROSS

1 Send skyward
5 Comic Foxx
9 Mimicked
13 Pittsburgh river
14 Fairy tale's penultimate word
15 Play with crayons
17 Broadway prize
18 Hold the deed to
19 Cord
20 Lamont Cranston
22 "__ care!"
23 Support
24 __ Culp Hobby (Eisenhower cabinet member)
25 Personnel slots
28 "__ Fidelis"
30 *Navidad* stuffed animal
32 Nosh
33 __-sutra
37 Dilettante
39 Broad-minded
41 The Flintstones' pet
42 The: Ger.
44 Convincing
45 Caught red-handed
48 Org.
49 North Dakota city
51 Layer of paint
53 Trivial
54 Leave out details
59 Follow
60 The Huxtables' youngest

61 Storied bear
62 Military strategy
63 Global speck
64 "The Lord __ shepherd . . ."
65 Luge
66 Bump into
67 Oolong and pekoe

DOWN

1 Mississippi senator
2 Klutz's exclamation
3 Excellent
4 30 Across filling
5 Back-to-normal process
6 Skirts
7 Aficionado

8 Sleuth Nancy
9 In effect
10 Volatile ones
11 Prufrock's creator
12 Actress Reed
16 Like Gen. Schwarzkopf
21 Waste maker
24 Of sight
25 Guitarist Hendrix
26 __ even keel
27 LSU site
29 __ *de tête* (headache)
30 Hippie digs
31 TV broadcast part
34 Mars' Greek counterpart

35 Jazzman Herbie
36 Computer key
38 Bro., e.g.
40 Dinghies
43 Hermit
46 Saw eye to eye
47 Scribble
49 End of a French film
50 Photographer Adams
52 To date
53 My: Fr.
54 Pessimistic
55 Skip
56 Bouquet container
57 Poet Lazarus
58 Sunbather's quest

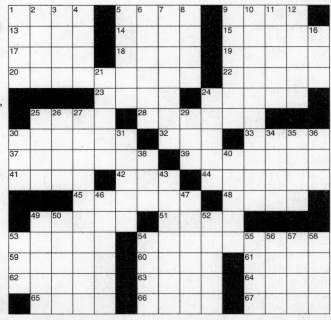

by Dean Niles

ACROSS

1 Small eatery
5 Boot attachment
10 Michael or Susannah
14 Winglike
15 __ ballerina
16 Sea east of the Caspian
17 Cook a cake
18 Career soldier
19 Extended-family member
20 "What Kind of Fool __?"
21 Left-handed patriot
23 Legendary lurer
25 Born: Fr.
26 Author Rand
27 Honest-man seeker
32 For short, for short
35 Ford or Els
36 "__ Como Va" (Santana tune)
37 Left-handed artist
41 Part of NATO
42 Like Seattle
43 Stir-fry pans
44 Oxford preserver
46 He defeated Spinks
48 "__ live and breathe!"
49 *Rhoda*, e.g.
53 Left-handed outlaw
58 Nemesis
59 *The Time Machine* race
60 Ancient Greek region
61 List shortener
62 Saint's image
63 Born first
64 Freight hauler
65 OJ substitute
66 Building level
67 Black crystal

DOWN

1 Gang of plotters
2 San Antonio mission
3 Hindu ascetic
4 Prior to
5 Peevish temper
6 Singer Lopez
7 Jazz phrase
8 Part of USA
9 Baseless suspicion
10 Gehrig or Mantle
11 Exam form
12 Rajah's mate
13 *Birth of a Nation* group
21 Memorable circumnavigator
22 Beersheba locale
24 Merit
27 Male bee
28 __ 500
29 It's verboten
30 Painter Jan van __
31 Twice *tres*
32 "Dear me!"
33 Alcott "woman"
34 Western tie
35 TV actress McClurg
38 Pretentious, in a way
39 Hen's teeth and blue moons
40 "Heads __, tails you lose"
45 London borough
46 Home for 27 Down
47 Trunk top
49 Mahre, for one
50 Regularly
51 Like the sea
52 Celluloid cat
53 "__ ever so . . ."
54 Actress Chase
55 Goofball
56 Romance novelist Victoria
57 Exo- opposite
61 "__ Beso" ('62 song)

WATER LOG

by Gerald R. Ferguson

ACROSS
1 Pistol packer of song
5 "Roger __" (radio phrase)
10 Small weight
14 Midmonth date
15 City on the Allegheny
16 Novelist Jaffe
17 Freckles and speckles
18 Established practice
19 Gabs
20 Part of the US/Canada border
22 Levin's namesakes
23 Happened next
24 Atlanta '96 org.
26 Room for Jekyll
27 Racer Mario
32 Cereal center
36 Capek play
37 Ebro *y* Orinoco
38 Ike's command: Abbr.
39 Whimper
40 TV spots
41 Midwestern capital
45 Sweet finales
47 Dashed (off)
48 Be obliged to
49 Benedict or Tom
53 Defect
56 Masters' __ *Anthology*

60 Hurry
61 Chan portrayer
62 Half of a Samoan town
63 Coloratura's piece
64 Bind again
65 Handy abbr.
66 Scout's shelter
67 Sample
68 Farmer's place

DOWN
1 Gnat
2 Bedeck
3 Doles out
4 Onslaughts
5 Aspiring
6 Victor Laszlo's wife
7 Plumbing problem
8 Actor Nicolas
9 "Gangway!"
10 Solid carbon dioxide
11 Crowd sound
12 "Lonely Boy" singer
13 Church service
21 Marsh duck
25 Mork's planet
27 Hoopster Gilmore
28 Illumination gas
29 Undeniable
30 Jethro of rock
31 Miffed
32 Metal fastener
33 Details handler
34 Fling

35 Part of CD
39 Walrus, for one
41 Clinch, with "up"
42 Bulk-mail ritual
43 Nobleman of Spain
44 Actor Jamie
46 "Who cares?"
50 Egg-shaped
51 Legitimate
52 Whimsical
53 Sigma Chi, e.g.
54 Tackle-box item
55 G __ "gnaw"
57 Defendant's answer
58 Morsels for mudders
59 "Step __!" ("Hurry!")

50 SERENITY

by Fred Piscop

ACROSS

1 Beethoven's *"Für __"*
6 Humorist Sahl
10 Vibraphonist Jackson
14 Filled a hold
15 More than
16 Anthem starter
17 COOL
20 Crocodile Dundee et al.
21 A Mouseketeer
22 On Soc. Sec., maybe
23 Pre-Christmas purchase
25 Driller's deg.
26 Wall St.'s locale
27 El __, TX
29 Aachen "alas"
32 Ronny Howard role
35 Actress Moran
37 Raid
39 CALM
42 Carpet fiber
43 Taiwanese dollar
44 Past due
45 Porker's pad
46 IOU signer
48 Some 45s
50 "__ been had!"
51 Malevolent
53 JFK's predecessor
56 Arête producer
60 Some spuds
62 COLLECTED
64 Words to Brutus
65 Concerning
66 Rich cake
67 Stinger
68 Nasty look
69 Actor Davis

DOWN

1 "Pomp and Circumstance" penner
2 Lash of oaters
3 That is: Lat.
4 Salty seven
5 Thing
6 Archie's dense pal
7 Egg cells
8 McEntire of country
9 Election-night topics
10 Specks
11 Doesn't exist
12 Café au __
13 Little feller
18 Japanese auto model
19 On __ (intermittently)
24 Gastronome
26 *Hud* star
28 "Diana" singer
29 Oratorio number
30 "I __ Get Started"
31 __ Park, NY
32 Singer Redding
33 Emily of etiquette
34 __-bitty
36 Abbott & Costello costar
38 Hooters
40 10th-century pope
41 Iroquoian language
47 Destructive insect
49 __ a draw (end up tied)
50 Freeze
52 Spiteful sort
53 Active ones
54 Tooth, in combinations
55 First name in cosmetics
56 Cultivated
57 "__ Smile Be Your Umbrella"
58 Bible book
59 Painter Magritte
61 Med. plans
63 Dr. __ (rap star)

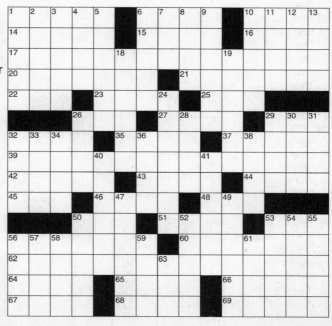

51 CATCH OF THE DAY

by Gregory E. Paul

ACROSS

1 Miner's tool
5 Elite group
10 Applaud
14 Traditional teachings
15 Shire of *Rocky*
16 Olympic sled
17 Gone fishing
18 Astrologist Sydney
19 Father of Eros
20 Apprehend
21 Vegas dish?
23 Calms down
25 Map features
26 Spinets
28 Newswoman Sawyer
30 L.A. athlete
31 Small gull
32 Telegram "."
36 Epoch
37 The catch of the day
40 Actress Thurman
41 Prepare salad
43 Atop
44 Deeply felt
46 Blender setting
48 Lessee
49 Moon project
52 Wise ones
53 New Orleans dish
56 Use a calculator
59 Succotash ingredient
60 Studio stand
61 Mr. Green's game
62 "Put a lid __!"
63 White poplar
64 Corridor
65 Hamilton's bills
66 Makes a home
67 At rest

DOWN

1 Blueprint
2 Keokuk's state
3 Baltimore dish
4 *Hazel* cartoonist
5 Pacific spots
6 Writer Janowitz et al.
7 Shem's son
8 Broadcasts
9 Walcott opponent
10 School groups
11 Novelist Alison
12 Intermediary
13 Cancún cash
21 Rolling Rock rival
22 Massachusetts cape
24 United
26 Realtor's map
27 1995 role for Kenneth Branagh
28 Crusoe's creator
29 Waffle or pig follower
31 Paper repairer
33 Deli dish
34 Foreshadowing
35 Divide
38 Dane, e.g.
39 Muralist Rivera
42 Wood strips
45 Wind dir.
47 Einstein's birthplace
48 Waiter's charge
49 Cravat kin
50 Brit's blower
51 Hatch of Utah
52 California fish
54 Comic Kaplan
55 Applications
57 Blunt
58 Marginal mark
61 Psi preceder

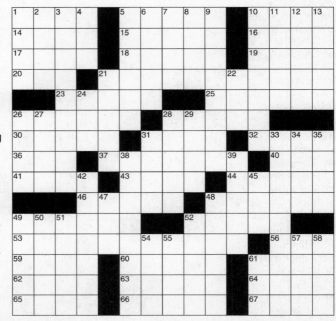

by Fred Piscop

ACROSS

1 Stop, at sea
6 "Nothing-but-net" sound
11 Maglie or Mineo
14 Decrees
15 __-surface missile
16 Method
17 Sir, in India
18 Cheap seats
20 Big name in software
22 "Go away!"
23 Bird call
26 Suffolk suffix
28 USAF bigwig
29 "__ want for Christmas . . ."
30 Coffee-and-chat group
33 Nabokov novel
34 Identical
35 "__ bagatelle!"
39 Makes a scene
41 Ant.
42 Used a sordino
43 __ *World Turns*
44 Speaker of baseball
46 Imbibe, in a way
47 Runner's destination
49 Hawaiian coastal area
50 Ripoff
53 Additional: Abbr.
54 Pencil part
56 Contentious one
58 One drop, roughly

60 No rocket scientist
62 Girl in an Everlys song
66 Writer Harper
67 Brings up
68 Outer, zoologically
69 ". . . __ I saw Elba"
70 Attack
71 Striped stinker

DOWN

1 Circular filler
2 Through
3 Innsbruck interjection
4 Old fogy
5 Verboten
6 Kemo __

7 Original "Golden Fleece" award presenter
8 Spleen
9 Equilibria
10 Pawn
11 Borg, for one
12 Home-run king
13 Air-freshener brand
19 Big cheese
21 Korean soldiers
23 *Meet John Doe* director
24 Radius neighbors
25 Black or Walker
27 Become involved
31 Taoism founder

32 Engine part
36 Moral nature
37 Come together
38 Mystery award
40 Part of a yen
45 Observed
48 *T.J. Hooker* actor
50 Mercury model
51 Colonial newsman
52 Go along
55 Reacts to yeast
57 Spanish river
59 Part of MIT
61 Some batteries
63 Actor Erwin
64 Scottish John
65 Wapiti

53 TO YOUR TASTE

by Fred Piscop

ACROSS
1 Casper, for one
6 Da __, Vietnam
10 Highest-rated
14 Oscar de la __
15 Where most people live
16 Role for Shirley
17 Northwestern highway
18 Some vehicles
19 Voyage
20 Fabled fruit
22 Big bag
23 Pittsburgh gridder
24 Cut off
26 Selves
28 __ Rosenkavalier
29 Envelope material
33 Of few words
37 "Whatever __ Wants"
38 Flows slowly
41 Yuletide
42 German autos
44 Noted sitcom couple
46 Summit
48 __ Ifni (Moroccan seaport)
49 Sock-drawer contents
53 Royal homes
58 Told a whopper
59 2/14 word
61 __ the Woods (Sondheim musical)
62 Arcade flub
63 Delegate
64 Wide-eyed
65 __ podrida

66 Parenthetical remark
67 Business partners, at times
68 Smeltery waste
69 Auberjonois et al.

DOWN
1 Tennis surface
2 Ancient serf
3 At the right time
4 Unremitting look
5 Tonsorial woes
6 The Guns of __
7 PDQ
8 Dressed to the __
9 Blotto

10 Diehard's destination?
11 Ballplayer's no-no
12 Strike down
13 Prerecorded
21 Millionaire host
25 Dog doc
27 Looks for
29 Day-__ (fluorescent paint)
30 __-eared (droopy)
31 Pub quaff
32 Vodka drinks
34 Generic defendant
35 Sun Yat-__
36 Golfer Ernie

39 Cost, so to speak
40 Mubarak's predecessor
43 Impresario Hurok
45 Perceive incorrectly
47 Green sauces
49 Alternate identity
50 One of the Fab Four
51 Board, as a bus
52 Hogwash
54 Preterit, e.g.
55 Linda of Alice
56 Chip away at
57 Eye sores
60 Actress Raines

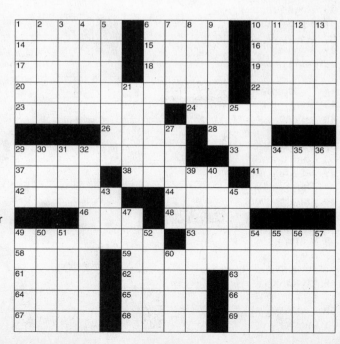

54

3 BY 5'S

by Charles Gersch

ACROSS
1 Unkempt
6 Prepare the presents
10 Drain element
14 Faye or Cooper
15 Pants measure
16 *Picket Fences* town
17 Hardware-store purchases
20 Word form for "strange"
21 __ *Jury* (Spillane novel)
22 Bit of land
23 Smallest part
25 Main highway
26 *Ecstasy* actress
29 See 10 Down
31 Squash variety
32 "Your majesty!"
33 Singer Irene
37 Bakery buy
40 Say no to
41 Ship part
42 Avian home
43 Even
44 "__ to grow on!"
45 Clergyman
49 Truffles, e.g.
51 Cast member
52 Confined
53 Cash drawer
57 1995 film, with *The*
60 Barnum client
61 Peruvian's ancestor
62 Heron's relative
63 Track info
64 Prepares Easter eggs
65 He played Grant

DOWN
1 Tailless feline
2 Nobelist Wiesel
3 Leo, for one
4 Erudite
5 Still
6 Judicial orders
7 Ballpark boundary
8 Tennis great
9 Millie or Socks
10 With 29 Across, custodial account
11 Esther of *Good Times*
12 Traffic-light color
13 Annoying
18 Münchhausen, for one
19 Charlie Parker's nickname
24 Shoreline flyer
25 Work without __ (take risks)
26 De __ (Marc Connelly character)
27 Soreness
28 Apollo 13's goal
30 Russian river
32 Cage's 1995 costar
33 Those owed
34 Plane-related
35 Showers
36 "Zip-__-Doo-Dah"
38 Running-motor sound
39 Loud sound
43 John Major, for one
44 Lit. collection
45 Cellist Casals
46 Pungent
47 Put up with
48 Lincoln in-laws
50 Fictional Mohican
52 Insignificant
54 Tennis star Lendl
55 *What's My __?*
56 Villainous look
58 Nod at Sotheby's, perhaps
59 Entertainment conglomerate

55 SCHOOL COLORS

by Gregory E. Paul

ACROSS

1 Singer Wooley
5 Stock unit
10 Smile broadly
14 Exude
15 Credo
16 Pasternak heroine
17 Spinner, e.g.
18 Bert's buddy
19 PC operator
20 Syracuse team
22 Golfer Calvin
23 Neighbor of Fla.
24 Scribbles
26 Distrustful
30 Compass part
32 Admiration
34 Neckline style
35 I saw: Lat.
39 Beaver's dad
40 Nautical direction
42 Object of worship
43 Plaintiff
44 Annoy
45 Moon goddess
47 __ Army (links legion)
50 Liability opposite
51 Energize
54 Bruins' #4
56 Heaps
57 Tulane team
63 Musical quality
64 Kicking partner
65 Plow pullers
66 Unique sort
67 Graf nemesis
68 Mixture
69 Capone catcher
70 Rhone feeder
71 Loupe, e.g.

DOWN

1 Fly unaided
2 From 0900 to 1000
3 Poet Pound
4 Existed
5 Gary product
6 Mr. Munster
7 Shakespeare's missus
8 Lapland animal
9 French season
10 Duke team
11 Three-legged stand
12 Alpine ridge
13 __-nest (hoax)
21 "What's Going On" singer
22 Office seeker, for short
25 *Waiting for Lefty* playwright
26 Wallace and Archer
27 Genesis name
28 To be, in Tours
29 Colgate team
31 Draw forth
33 Home of the Black Bears
36 May 15, e.g.
37 Fully cooked
38 "__ a Song Go . . ."
41 Frito-Lay's competitor
46 Have coming
48 Campers, for short
49 At all
51 Rocker John
52 Not a soul
53 Bowler's haunt
55 Dodger great
58 Incense
59 New Zealand export
60 Wheel holder
61 Blood vessel
62 NASA chimp
64 "__ live and breathe!"

56 SAY AAH

by Dean Niles

ACROSS

1 Loathe
5 Canned meat
9 Kind of fastener
14 Chester ___ Arthur
15 "And here it is!"
16 Scarlett's surname
17 Sweet stuff
19 Father Damien's charge
20 Flabbergasts
21 Senator Simon's trademark
22 Vitamin-label initials
23 Skirt length
24 Fawn of film
28 Father of 24 Across
30 Salamander
34 Hardens by exposure
36 Like some deals
37 Merriment
38 Sky sight
39 Ohio river
41 Ridicule
42 Ancient Greek city
43 Hem-haw link
44 Wheat component
46 Take it easy
47 Ship mates
49 Board material
50 Cod cousin
52 Not vert.
54 Holds responsible
57 Lives it up
62 Flushed
63 Sweet stuff
64 Expiate, with "for"
65 Roll spread
66 Math course
67 Inclinations
68 Aquatic bird
69 Hops kiln

DOWN

1 Joke response
2 "Dear me!"
3 Sharp on the tongue
4 Word form for "within"
5 Continue in force
6 Bamboo eaters
7 Interjects
8 Merry month
9 Wise one
10 Sweet stuff
11 Absorbed
12 ". . . ___ saw Elba"
13 Piece of merchandise
18 Big name in physics
21 Hotshot
23 Term of respect
24 Tour de France entrant
25 Doddering
26 Hushes
27 Aromatic stuff
29 Barter
31 Type type
32 Sociologist Max
33 Really small
35 Clobbers
40 Concerning
45 The king, in France
48 Trawler
51 Yellow-fever mosquito
53 Acrylic fiber
54 Gossip
55 Beer choice
56 English river
57 Kid-lit king
58 Until
59 Marsh bird
60 Amer. Anglican
61 Certain NCO
63 Whole bunch

PUNISHING

by Dean Niles

ACROSS

1 First name on jeans
5 Arp's genre
9 Manicotti, e.g.
14 Minute particle
15 Oodles
16 *Laugh-In* name
17 Very sharp
19 Muse of poetry
20 The Big Apple: Abbr.
21 "This __ joke!"
22 __ down the hatches
23 Contemptible one
25 __ *in the Hat*
27 Hodges or Gerard
28 "Put a lid on it!"
29 Curve shape
32 Actress Hayes
35 *Jane* __
36 Guitar device
37 Juice fruits
39 Footrest
41 History
42 "Put __ writing!"
44 Rash
45 Boy or girl ending
46 Genesis site
47 Computer monitor: Abbr.
48 Valentine exchangers
50 Pastoral
54 Chalkboard tool
56 Takes advantage
58 Latin I verb
59 Screened again

60 Befuddled
62 Dial device
63 Not colorful
64 Victorian prime minister
65 Expedite
66 The A in B.A.
67 Paris airport

DOWN

1 Grassy areas
2 Gas additive
3 Tenor or bass
4 Mischievous sprite
5 Distressed one of old films
6 Shepard of NASA
7 Wit Parker

8 ABA member
9 Evangelize
10 Heart line
11 Special forces
12 London gallery
13 Bartlett's abbr.
18 Fabric strengthener
22 Hem in
24 FBI guy
26 A Great Lake
30 Tiff
31 Walkman maker
32 Western Indian
33 Time intervals
34 Cowboy hero

35 Acid + alcohol result
36 Paint layers
38 Diving duck
40 Songbird
43 Narrow-minded
46 Made smooth
47 Fancy pancakes
49 Siouan language
51 Slim down
52 Force on
53 With modesty
54 Work units
55 Gather the crop
57 Shaker contents
60 Warm spot
61 Mil. address

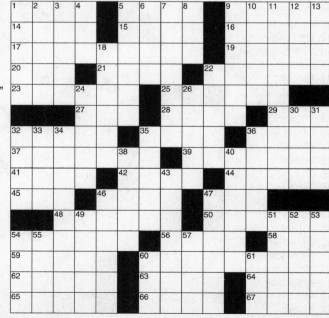

CLUMSY

by Bob Lubbers

ACROSS

1 Tease
4 Dollop
7 Alan of *M*A*S*H*
11 Pitcher's stat
12 Fruit trees
16 Boxer Spinks
17 Class outings
19 Deposed Ugandan
20 Soup alternative
21 Last bits
23 Single
24 Plead
26 __ *Even With Dad* (1994 film)
28 Drain
31 Scale pair
33 *Sturm __ Drang*
34 Winter fall
37 Barber's gear
40 *The Numerals* painter
41 Belgian Congo, later
43 Acting part
44 Factions
46 Wood smoother
48 With it
49 True
50 Tippler
51 Pension payee
54 __ *culpa*
56 Guitarist Montgomery
57 Japanese-American
59 Mule kin
63 Felled
65 Doesn't succeed
67 Bard's river
68 Wrestle
69 Estuary
70 Cat sound
71 Tote (up)
72 Sawbuck

DOWN

1 NBA officials
2 Siepi solo
3 Highlander
4 Shakes
5 Model Carol
6 Hoopster Larry
7 __ carte
8 Candy bits
9 "Nothing __!"
10 Baxter or Boleyn
13 Stately dances?
14 Dueling sword
15 Certain noncom: Abbr.
18 Igor's domain
22 Erwin et al.
25 Saxophonist Stan
27 Mural starter
28 __ *Gotta Have It* (Lee film)
29 Bern's river
30 Acts amorously
32 Emu cousins
35 "__ all hang out!"
36 Sea eagle
38 Butter sub
39 Jaunty
42 Balled cheese
45 Make yarn
47 Glad
51 Actor Christopher
52 Fissure
53 Jacob's brother
55 Fire residue
56 "Kapow!"
58 Rick's love
60 Type
61 Albany-to-Buffalo canal
62 Comic Freberg
64 Wind dir.
66 Vended: Abbr.

TRUE COLORS

by Dean Niles

ACROSS

1 Acreage
5 Wine valley
9 "Arrivederci, __"
13 Sore spot
14 Straws in the wind
16 Vice
17 "Take __ leave it!"
18 Coffee choice
19 Pre-Easter season
20 Hypocritical principle
23 Nightwear
24 __-Mex cuisine
25 Songlike passage
29 Fortune-teller
31 Bake-sale org.
34 Seed pod
35 Great period for business
38 "Deutschland über __"
40 Table part
41 Tall tales
42 Patriotic songs
45 Corporate symbol
46 Rugrat
47 Wing-shaped
48 Hotel name
50 Thimbleful
51 Singing syllable
52 World Series participants
60 __ mater
61 Physicist Marie
62 Kerrigan leap
63 Hairdo
64 Smart __ (wise guy)
65 Actress Lollobrigida

66 Caesarean query
67 Sediment
68 Put away

DOWN

1 Set down
2 Word form for "eight"
3 You, once
4 Certain Slav
5 Rhinoplasty
6 Put together
7 Confined
8 "Diana" singer
9 Take five
10 Concluded
11 Pay attention to
12 Model Carol
15 South Carolina river

21 Pre-CD purchases
22 Irish county seat
25 To the rear, nautically
26 Norse chieftain
27 __ ease (awkward)
28 Designer Cassini
29 Scornful look
30 B&O job
31 '92 candidate
32 Dramatic dance
33 Fiery crime
36 Thomas __ Edison
37 "__ come back now!"

39 Rustic fellow
43 Variety of wool
44 Expresses horror
49 Oddjob's creator
50 Big mess
51 Think __ about (reconsider)
52 Garden area
53 Send forth
54 __ and void
55 Family chart
56 Keeps on one's case
57 Stadium sign
58 Gambling town
59 Deli dish
60 Hotshot aviator

by Norma Steinberg

ACROSS

1 Eye covers
5 Dred Scott, e.g.
10 Bandstand equipment
14 *The King* __
15 Indian spice
16 Yarn
17 Patient's status
20 Chinese sauce
21 United, in France
22 Bird house
23 Club offering?
24 Mamie's predecessor
26 In any way
29 Nautical
33 Poet Teasdale
34 Worries
35 John __ Passos
36 Let one's hair down
40 Geologic period
41 Broadway lights
42 Swiss artist
43 Stocking style
45 Takes five
46 Adjutant
47 Oolong et al.
49 Colonial Quaker
51 Long skirt
52 Buscaglia or Gorcey
55 Protest formally
59 Sheriff Taylor's boy
60 Configuration
61 Matthew's former name
62 Suds
63 Flower part
64 Fellows

DOWN

1 Annie Laurie, for one
2 Long-division word
3 6/6/44
4 Bro or sis
5 Emotional confrontation
6 Desi's daughter
7 Famous cookie maker
8 Sportscaster Scully
9 Movie's last word
10 Warrant
11 "__ oui!"
12 Story line
13 Hatch or Boxer: Abbr.
18 Eye of the storm
19 Stick to one's guns
23 Word before hand or rags
24 Points
25 ". . . __ saw Elba"
26 Long-eared equines
27 California/ Nevada lake
28 Madison Square Garden, e.g.
29 Water carriers
30 Role models
31 Contemporary of Degas
32 Curvy letters
34 Picked out
37 Skate style
38 Prerequisite
39 Turner and Eisenhower
44 "Away in a __"
45 Racetrack fence
47 Buccaneers' home
48 Kick out
49 Karol Wojtyla's title
50 Mrs. Ernie Kovacs
51 Castle protector
52 Stead
53 Covetousness
54 Singer Redding
55 Toss
56 Snake
57 Fidel's lieutenant
58 HS math

61 FOWL PLAY

by Rich Norris

ACROSS

1 Track circuits
5 Rainbows
9 Aug. and Sept.
12 Thick-pile carpets
14 Letter opener
15 Kick
16 Sign of fear
18 Vicinity
19 Pop's bro
20 Polite refusal
21 Knight wear
22 Coll. hoops tourney
23 Easy mark
25 North Atlantic islands
27 Greek markets
28 Hospital supplies
29 Ventriloquist Lewis
32 Farm enclosure
33 Harassed, in a way
37 __ gratia artis
40 Stadium sounds
41 "Fernando" singing group
45 Employ, as an attorney
47 Morality tales
49 Trifling amount
53 Gore and Capp
54 Sword parts
55 Did a maintenance chore
56 OSS successor
57 Perry's creator
58 Habit-breaking method

60 Rex or Donna
61 "That's clear!"
62 Complaint
63 Lith., once
64 Pre-1959 Hawaii: Abbr.
65 Barney's pal

DOWN

1 Inlets
2 Worry (about)
3 Exam overseer
4 Airline to Stockholm
5 Scorched
6 Send the check
7 Isle in Naples Bay
8 Grads-to-be: Abbr.
9 Speaks low
10 Ball game variant
11 Ringo's real last name
13 Meaning
15 TV announcer Don
17 Wood: Fr.
21 Longhorn rival
24 Stoolie, in Sussex
26 Stadium sound
29 Sauna locale
30 That girl
31 Cooling appliances: Abbr.
34 Estrada and Satie
35 Not any

36 Apply lightly
37 Cupid et al.
38 Employs again
39 Meara's partner
42 More soiled
43 Accept as truth
44 Analyzed, as ore
46 Pretended
47 Stocking fillers
48 Make sense
50 Lasso end
51 Secretary, at times
52 Church figure
58 Townsman, for short
59 Ump's kin

LONG QUINTET

by Mary Brindamour

ACROSS
1. __ Beach, FL
5. Insecticides: Abbr.
9. Fashion magazine
13. Enthusiasm
14. Political power
15. Null's partner
16. Oriole's home
17. Small egg
18. Writer Bombeck
19. Quixote's quest
22. Butter quantity
23. Dykstra or Kravitz
24. Flowering plant
27. DDE's opponent
28. Regarding
32. Coral deposit
33. In the past
34. Molecular relative
35. One of a Latin trio
36. __ Haute, IN
38. Marry, for some
39. Golf club
41. Postal Creed word
42. Epithet for Athena
43. Facial contortion
44. NASA assent
45. Not active
46. Dieter's concern
48. Embellish
49. Endorse, in a way
56. Bear's cave
57. Religious worshipers
58. Runner's goal
59. Vocal
60. Sea eagles
61. Sicilian spouter
62. Work monotonously
63. M.B.A. and Ph.D.
64. Finger tip

DOWN
1. Latin I word
2. Basic: Abbr.
3. Coarse file
4. Overjoyed
5. 556, in old Rome
6. Gambler's choice
7. Veil materials
8. Dutch painter
9. Sporadically
10. Traditional knowledge
11. Peruvian capital
12. Party cheese
14. Market price
20. Kenny G's instrument
21. Genetic codes: Abbr.
24. Baby buggies
25. Virile type
26. Consumer's option
27. ID information
29. Novelist Zola
30. At no time
31. Something special
33. Took sustenance
34. Comparative suffix
37. Korean soldier
40. Mideast country
44. Looking intently
45. Altar response
47. Twiddled one's thumbs
48. Carter and Vanderbilt
49. Hog feed
50. Hoopster Monroe
51. Luigi's farewell
52. Parisian summers
53. Little bit
54. Former Atlanta arena
55. Actress Patricia

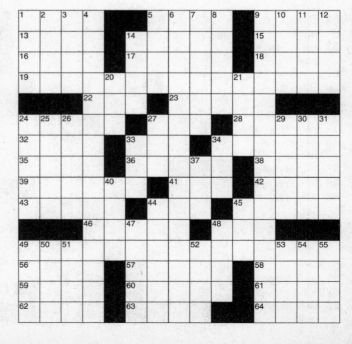

63 MATCHING PAIRS

by Thomas W. Schier

ACROSS
1 Mosque figure
5 Receive enthusiastically
10 Arp's style
14 Sitar music
15 __ acid (organic compound)
16 North Carolina university
17 Children's teaching innovator
20 Stradivari's teacher
21 Carry
22 Top 40 song
23 Cinema canine
26 Cornell locale
28 Fifth Dimension singer
33 Word form for "outer"
34 __ Arden
35 Swedish inventor
39 School book
41 Fouled up
43 Surreal artist
44 So far
46 Slugger Hank
48 Squealer
49 Yankees' #7
52 Wrist-related
55 Fifth-century pope
56 Mature
57 Narrow inlets
60 Fibber of old radio
64 Law & Order actor
68 The Time Machine people

69 Pacific island
70 Green land
71 Give for a bit
72 Detroit player
73 Imitated

DOWN
1 __ la Douce
2 Sir's counterpart
3 Taj Mahal city
4 Rum drink
5 On the __ (fleeing)
6 I love: Lat.
7 Quaff quantity
8 "For __ us a child . . ."
9 Of verse
10 __ Plaines, IL
11 Ho's hello

12 Column type
13 Singer Baker
18 Usher's beat
19 Attack
24 Actress Daly
25 Eskimo parka
27 Parka adjunct
28 "I never __ man I . . ."
29 Hatchets
30 Theater name
31 Singer Carmen
32 Ladd or Tiegs
36 Homer's kid
37 Mideast airline
38 Lo-fat
40 Office fill-in
42 Rotunda topper

45 Pageant prop
47 Wynonna's mom
50 Customer
51 Ancient Asia Minor city
52 Bumpy beast
53 Like gymnasts
54 Spy work, for short
58 Jai __
59 Self-satisfied
61 Stagehand
62 French 101 verb
63 Looked at
65 Laid low
66 Boxcar cargo
67 Capek drama

64 LOCATION SHOTS

by Dean Niles

ACROSS

1 Entranced
5 Big name in insurance
10 __ mecum (handbook)
14 Czech river
15 Essays
16 Seed cover
17 1984 movie
19 Actor Neeson
20 Late morning
21 Principles
23 Varnish ingredient
24 Contaminate
27 1981 movie
32 Rotation letters
35 Percolates
36 Concerning
37 Makes true
39 Region of Spain
41 Options list
42 Physicist Nikola
45 French connections
46 1936 movie
50 Component
51 Muggy
55 Holiday rival
58 Adjust the guitar again
59 Declare openly
60 1942 movie
64 Contribute
65 Shiraz native
66 Composer __-Carlo Menotti
67 Put to work
68 Oversized book
69 Laborer of old

DOWN

1 Gallup rival
2 Allan-__
3 Fathers of France
4 Small stuff
5 Notice abbr.
6 Afore
7 Ducats, informally
8 Teachers' grp.
9 St. Francis of __
10 Sweet orange
11 *Fidelio* feature
12 Phone feature, once
13 *Desire Under the* __
18 Forwarded
22 Mr. Severinsen
24 Poet Octavio
25 A person
26 "__ Too Late" (Carole King tune)
28 Victoria de __ Angeles
29 *Picnic* playwright
30 Gait
31 Cravings
32 St. Louis team
33 Guilty or not guilty
34 N. Dak. neighbor
38 Laughed heartily
39 Jolson and Jarreau
40 *Silent Spring* author Carson
42 Cable station
43 Author Umberto
44 *To __ With Love*
47 Groovy
48 Yellow-flowered shrub
49 Power failure
52 Some bonds
53 Ancient Peruvian
54 Colonial diplomat Silas
55 Aunt Millie's rival
56 Rara __
57 Ambulate
58 Baseball stats
61 __ Deco
62 Maglie or Mineo
63 Santa __, CA

65 ON COURSE

by Bob Lubbers

ACROSS

1 Careless
5 Leather band
10 British streetcar
14 Grid great Graham
15 __ facie
16 Aviation word form
17 Thrust
18 Light beam
19 *Kiss Me, __*
20 CADDY
23 Addams cousin
24 Model-train name
28 Hunger pains
31 Some Indonesians
33 __ Jessica Parker
34 Become united
35 Simile center
36 TEE
40 Massachusetts cape
41 Fill
42 High schoolers
43 Atomic piles
46 Ladd classic
47 Close up again
48 '60s ring king
49 TRAP
56 Big brass
59 Hackneyed
60 Run in neutral
61 Software buyer
62 Annoy
63 Beatty and Rorem
64 Jokes
65 Scorches
66 Former Moscow Agency

DOWN

1 Diva Ponselle
2 Aleutian island
3 Right away, in the ER
4 Rail rider
5 Takes off
6 Area
7 Peril
8 "Hallelujah!" follower
9 Side-by-side
10 Hire
11 Actor Stephen
12 Skilled workmanship
13 A Stooge
21 Darkness
22 1002, to Caesar
25 Spruce up
26 Ancient ascetic
27 Norman and Edward
28 Kansas Indian
29 Fight sites
30 Bobbsey girl
31 __ in (meddles)
32 North Carolina county
33 Bart or Kay
34 Dread
37 Sets apart
38 Moral discipline
39 Midday quaff
44 Lebanese trees
45 Old salt
46 Rains ice
48 __ Is Born
50 *"Dies __"*
51 Naldi of the silents
52 Hue
53 Brainstorm
54 Buick rival
55 Nitti nemesis
56 Haul
57 "Born in the __"
58 Beseech

by Dean Niles

ACROSS

1 Heavenly strings
5 Schism
9 Doled (out)
14 USA part
15 Memo words
16 Breathing
17 Burt's ex
18 Sly as __
19 More logical
20 Completely, in the Navy
23 Put into law
24 Traveler's rider
25 "__ luego"
28 Hoppers
30 Aggregate
33 .33333 . . .
35 Letter abbr.
36 Tiny insect
37 Across
40 Exhaust
41 Jack of *Barney Miller*
42 *My __ With Andre*
43 Watched Junior
44 Lettuce varieties
46 Tractor name
47 USAF unit
48 Lacking
50 Meteoric rise
57 More than miffed
58 "Three men in __"
59 "I could __ horse"
60 Playing marble
61 Like some horror films
62 French silk center
63 Cotton worker
64 Iowa State home
65 Moistens, in a way

DOWN

1 Equal share
2 Eros
3 Clinton cabinet member
4 Broadcasting period
5 Ranchero's rope
6 Spoil
7 Completely
8 Written material
9 ". . . huddled __ yearning . . ."
10 Thrill
11 Trident feature
12 At all
13 Father-daughter acting name
21 Tie-up
22 Ireland, affectionately
25 Sword holders
26 Open-air malls
27 Underfunded
29 Likely
30 Actress Hasso
31 King Arthur's father
32 Scotland yard?
34 Italian director
36 Area fraught with danger
38 Watch pocket
39 Unencumbered with
44 With less tread
45 Sewing seam
47 Do in
49 Namesakes of a Shakespearean sot
50 Bodybuilder's bane
51 Latvian capital
52 Race track
53 Epic tale
54 Mirthful Martha
55 Put away
56 Summer shades

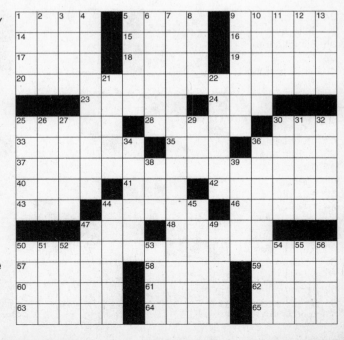

FULL OF BALONEY

by Gerald R. Ferguson

ACROSS
1 Locket feature
6 Shooting game
10 Kemo __
14 Ring boundaries
15 Simplify
16 Fearsome dinosaur, briefly
17 Claptrap
19 Yorkshire river
20 Stately home
21 Abandon
23 Navigator's dir.
24 Cable choice
26 Baste a bit
27 Bafflegab
33 Day, in Dijon
36 The Continent: Abbr.
37 Frightening
38 Pluralizers
40 Relig. school
41 Dimwitted
42 Armada
43 "__ to Pieces" (1965 song)
44 Witnessed
45 Symbol of untruth
49 Negative vote
50 Convened
51 Twaddle
54 Sweet treat
58 Verdi opera
60 Julio Iglesias song
61 Gibberish
65 Ruinous thing
66 Gull cousin
67 Indian royalty
68 Queued up
69 Invasion
70 British guns

DOWN
1 French pancake
2 Miller's salesman
3 IBM rival
4 __ good example
5 Hitchcock thriller
6 GM car
7 Dory accessory
8 Hallucinogen
9 Came clean, with "up"
10 Asterisk
11 58 Across solo
12 Aare city
13 Made one's mark
18 He was Friday
22 Jacket material
25 Nutritionist's concern
26 Pulpit orations
27 Plato's tongue
28 "¡Hasta __!"
29 Gaggle group
30 Sarah __ Jewett
31 Seine tributary
32 Sharp
33 Mutt's pal
34 Cold capital
35 Internet patron
39 Office transcriber
46 Temper
47 London lockup
48 Says
51 Aircraft
52 Paar predecessor
53 Jabs
54 Raisin cake
55 General Bradley
56 Taboo
57 Percolate
59 State of France
62 Man-mouse link
63 Cycle start
64 Garden area

68 NOUN YOU SEE IT

by Dean Niles

ACROSS

1 Mexican munchies
6 Noted pediatrician
11 Time-shifting device
14 Disconcert
15 Mr. Television
16 __ mode
17 Time off
19 One of two Chaneys
20 Competed
21 "Tiny" singer
22 Clobber
23 Actor Lahr
25 Righteous Brothers tune
27 Bear
31 __ Khan
32 Baby powder
33 Lake of talk
35 Cut, in a way
38 Everywhere
42 Actress Arthur
43 Startle
44 Part of 64 Across
45 Energy
46 Senior's keepsake
49 Grad-school offering
53 Swiss artist
54 Fuddy-duddy
55 Notwithstanding, informally
57 Sale site
61 High-proof spirit
62 Doohickey
64 Wire service
65 Moore of stew
66 School for Stendhal
67 And like that: Abbr.
68 Reporter's coup
69 Steel rod

DOWN

1 Timothy Hutton movie
2 Help feloniously
3 Mystery writer John Dickson
4 Veal dish
5 Pickup tool
6 Loan agcy.
7 Hit with stones
8 "Live Free __"
9 Get-together
10 Largo or Biscayne
11 "Grease" singer
12 Obscure
13 Extent
18 Geek
22 Porker's pad
24 __ firma
26 Radar spot
27 Pierce
28 Hearty
29 Cooking pot
30 Swank
34 Effrontery
35 __ War (racehorse)
36 Numerical prefix
37 Bubbly bandleader
39 Puffed-up
40 Showing concern
41 Flamboyant pianist
45 Turn, in a way
47 Aquatic organism
48 Pipe tool
49 Metal-mold opening
50 Blow up
51 Ape or parrot
52 Horned mammal
56 Informed (about)
58 "Get __" ('58 tune)
59 __ monster
60 German river
62 6-pt. scores
63 Swindle

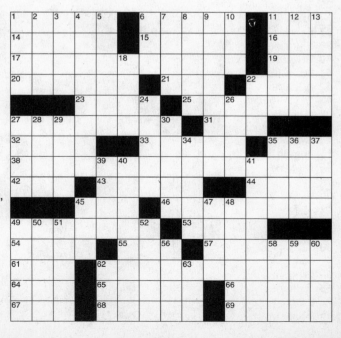

69 BODY BLOWS

by Randolph Ross

ACROSS

1 Islamic priest
5 Charlie Brown expletive
9 Annex
14 Major story
15 Computer symbol
16 Talk idly
17 Kids' cereal
18 Greek colonnade
19 Freak out
20 Symbol of betrayal
23 From __ Z
24 Org. once headed by George Bush
25 Kiss
33 Roman goddesses
34 Large ref. work
35 They're on the books
37 Collar types
38 Shake up
39 Principle
40 Have supper
41 Spanish article
42 __ Rogers St. Johns
43 Ambition
47 Cow-feteria
48 Tokyo, originally
49 Light punishment
57 Aglow
58 Music to a comic
59 German region
61 Woody Allen film
62 State strongly
63 Nautical adverb
64 Little pests
65 Exigency
66 Pier

DOWN

1 Special suffix
2 Grade
3 Opposed to, informally
4 Long dress
5 __ the occasion
6 Director's call
7 Betty Boop, e.g.
8 Grabber
9 Attractiveness
10 Unexciting
11 Actress Wynter
12 Aural
13 Violin part
21 Charlatans
22 Got going
25 Got rid of
26 Recurring theme
27 Rice-__
28 Rattan artisan
29 Salute with drink
30 __ France (Former French province)
31 Expert group
32 Blow up
36 Corset stiffener
38 Swift fellow
39 Little drum
41 Bank attachment
44 Emulates Romeo and Juliet
45 Titter
46 Albert or Arnold
49 Shut loudly
50 Leslie Caron role
51 Busy
52 Shade of purple
53 Retain
54 OPEC member
55 *Enterprise* name
56 "Take __ Train"
60 Alejandro or Fernando

SPEAKING XHOSA

by Matt Gaffney

ACROSS

1 Stocky marsupial
7 "Harrumph!"
10 Strike callers
14 Shirley, in *Terms of Endearment*
15 Cable choice
16 Do some budget-cutting
17 DC
19 Skating jump
20 Barnaby Jones portrayer
21 Pre-game music
23 Plant swelling
26 Lessen
28 Stadium cousin
29 Ankle-length
30 Caspian feeder
31 Oolong et al.
32 Kurt Waldheim's predecessor
34 Not granted
36 Wet expanse
37 List starter
39 Turn on the charm
40 Obstacle, in a way
43 __ in (heralds)
46 Woodstock companion
48 Concerning
49 Earned
51 Staff marking
52 Available
53 Actress Irving
54 Some e-mail
55 Ladle, e.g.
57 McEnroe's ex
59 Czech Olympian Zátopek
60 Albanian leader, 1944-85
65 Music medium
66 Fission products
67 Threw in the towel
68 Enjoy the snow
69 It's about 80% nitrogen
70 Nervous

DOWN

1 Used to be
2 Arles assent
3 Mystery man
4 Czech region
5 Resort island
6 Vacation by-products
7 Spoil
8 Employ
9 Mock fanfare
10 Cornered
11 '80s cyber-character
12 Adorns (oneself)
13 Alabama River city
18 Antelope playmate
22 Iroquois, e.g.
23 Some cassowaries
24 See
25 Car part
27 Botched
30 *The __ Reader* (literary mag)
33 Pessimist's problem
35 Wine attribute
38 Writer Bombeck
41 Plotting
42 Tournament exemptions
44 Forsook paper clips
45 Russian for "self-boiler"
47 Bob Marley song
48 Muppets drummer
50 A little force
52 *Waiting for Lefty* playwright
54 Naval historian
56 Shah name
58 Thus
61 Coveted NCAA ranking
62 Signed, perhaps
63 Clasp
64 Boor

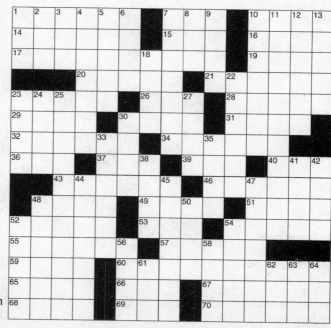

CHRISTMAS IN JULY

by Dean Niles

ACROSS

1 Smeltery leftover
5 Burden
9 Boat or plane
14 TV actress Williams
15 Hungarian leader Nagy
16 Madagascar primate
17 Paris airport
18 Actress Patricia
19 Yellowish white
20 Food mishap
23 Diverting
24 Passbook abbr.
25 Turns abruptly
30 Time period
32 *Inter* __
34 First one counted
35 Lts.' school
37 Roughly forever
38 Water pipe
39 Vacillate
43 Milky quartz
44 The third degree?
45 Island in a stream
46 Waffle brand
47 Beef concoction
49 Casino city, for short
53 Director Tarantino
55 Record label
57 Model Carol
58 Meringue-top dessert
61 Kids' entertainer
65 Burglar
66 Ski lift
67 Certain postings
68 Pulitzer author Robert __ Butler
69 Soda-shop offering
70 Video-display element
71 Meat-inspecting agcy.
72 Sponsorship

DOWN

1 Derides, with "at"
2 Thrash
3 Actress Dahl
4 "Ain't That Peculiar" singer
5 Bedding
6 Code of silence
7 Breed of horse
8 Grandeur, often
9 Singer Patsy
10 Title for Dr. King
11 Latin lover's verb
12 Sable or mink
13 Essay
21 Exactly nothing
22 African republic
26 Distant
27 Cutlet meat
28 Sooner city
29 Dictionary abbr.
31 __ broil (steak choice)
33 Sales prospects
36 Mrs. Ponti
39 Sauce brand
40 Yen
41 Courteous remark
42 Courteous
43 Et __ (footnote abbr.)
48 Equivocated
50 Blowhard
51 Acid neutralizer
52 Kicks off
54 Treasury offering
56 __ Carta
59 Lampreys
60 "Ma! (He's Making Eyes __)"
61 Agent
62 "Who __ to say?"
63 Office output
64 "Fee, __, foe, fum . . ."

BACK TO WOODSTOCK

by Fred Piscop

ACROSS
1 Part of L.A.
4 __ *Three Lives*
8 Antarctic sea
12 Prefix for center
13 "Well, I __!"
15 Musical pace
16 *The Novel of the Future* writer
17 Woodstock wear
19 Does a vet's chore
21 Banishes
22 Artoo Detoo's owner
23 Granular snows
24 Woodstock wear
29 Redact
30 Party
31 Seer's card
33 Sleep phenom.
34 Sculpted form
39 Ebbets Field great
42 Do
43 Woodstock wear
46 Social stratum
47 Ring sites?
48 Shots at the majors
50 Board with a thumbhole
53 Woodstock wear
55 Work unit
56 China name
57 Nine, in combinations
58 __ trade (fashion industry)

59 Parisian parent
60 Williams and Danson
61 Mole, for one

DOWN
1 Do a bank job
2 Role for Ronny
3 Oil company with a dinosaur logo
4 Hurting
5 Margins
6 Spacewalks, to NASA
7 Calendar abbr.
8 Kick out
9 Shadows: Fr.
10 Stage illumination
11 Peruvian coins

14 Coach Auerbach
15 Compose, in a way
18 Smell, e.g.
20 Slowly, on a score
24 Garner
25 Dietary initials
26 Motown founder
27 City on the Meuse
28 Dangerous partner
32 Idiot box
35 Earthy color
36 Revels noisily
37 Francis Drake title

38 Frequently, in poetry
40 Shelley's "__ the West Wind"
41 Really ticked
43 Singer Dayne
44 Wagnerian heroine
45 Hot sauces
46 Fancy flapjack
48 1/2 fl. oz.
49 __-Foy, Que.
50 Corn concoction
51 It may be cheese-filled
52 Like some waffles
54 Blaster's need

73 FISH OUT OF WATER

by Rose White

ACROSS

1 Tax preparer: Abbr.
4 Wave tops
8 Less distant
14 Scene stealer
15 Exclamation of surprise
16 Alert again
17 Cold War phenomenon
19 Kampala's country
20 Stunt sport
22 Lion coiffure
23 Still
24 Taylor's nickname
27 Thin margin
32 Russo of *Outbreak*
33 Part of TGIF
36 Sign of the future
37 Devout
38 Pioneer's motto
42 Bottomless pit
43 *In __ veritas*
44 *The Daughter of Time* novelist
45 Father
46 Grass sign
49 __ Paulo
50 Corn holder
51 Quickly, for short
55 "The Twist" singer
61 Inuit
63 Humidifier output
64 Cotton pest
65 Soft drink
66 Prevaricate
67 Lengthen
68 Baseball manager Felipe
69 Writer Kesey

DOWN

1 Wide fissure
2 Hooded jacket
3 Jordan's capital
4 Treat meat
5 Jezebel's husband
6 Somewhat, musically
7 Where the Mets play
8 Less refined
9 On the level
10 Gulf off Iran
11 Specify
12 Result
13 Cereal-box info: Abbr.
18 Simmer slowly
21 Whiskey grain
25 Occupied
26 Like salsa
28 One of the Cartwrights
29 Mischievous child
30 Bishop's domain
31 Rogue
32 Tease
33 Cardplayer's comment
34 Shinbone
35 Rise rapidly
37 College teacher, casually
39 WNW opposite
40 Kenyan runner Keino
41 Yoko __
46 German spirit
47 Decline
48 True statement
50 Chili spice
52 Slink
53 Eagle's nest
54 Groom
56 Hotbed of activity
57 Village People song
58 Unresponsive
59 City near Mauna Loa
60 Birthright seller
61 Ram's mate
62 Gender

VEGGIE ANATOMY

by Patrick Jordan

ACROSS

1 '92 rival of Bill and George
5 Pack tightly
9 Descendant
14 "Now __ me down . . ."
15 Breathing sound
16 TV announcer Don
17 Convent room
18 "Self" starter
19 Galahad's getup
20 Boxer feature
23 Undamaged
24 Stuff to the gills
25 Cave-painting subject
28 *No Exit* author
32 Be disputatious
35 He reached his peak
37 Shocking swimmer
38 Feeble notions
42 Track transaction
43 Espied
44 Move obliquely
45 Rough design
48 Begrimes
50 Baldwin of *The Shadow*
52 Most agreeable
56 Translucent stationery
60 Silverstein et al.
61 Galileo's birthplace
62 Actor Calhoun
63 Yes follower
64 Settled down
65 CCII x III
66 Actor James
67 Pinocchio's polygraph
68 Worn out

DOWN

1 Christina of *The Addams Family*
2 New York city
3 Port __ cheese
4 Milk/cider drink
5 Some county fair displays
6 Actor Julia
7 Choir voice
8 Feline lines
9 Conqueror of Athens
10 Profession
11 Mlle. la Douce
12 Olfactory offense
13 Postal Creed word
21 More arctic
22 Went (in) gradually
26 Bee's grandnephew
27 Dressed to the __
29 Sore, with "off"
30 Tangible
31 Other
32 PD alerts
33 Offend the nose
34 Box-office receipts
36 Lottolike game
39 Pale
40 New York town
41 Poker-hand rejects
46 Followed, à la Spade
47 Does the finale
49 Hereditary
51 Where *Booknotes* may be seen
53 Geologic term
54 Electronic mechanism
55 "Have a taste!"
56 Louisville's river
57 Rex's tec
58 Metric unit, briefly
59 Egyptian deity
60 Compass dir.

AFTER SEVEN

by Bob Lubbers

ACROSS

1 Rec rooms
5 Extra-base hit
11 __ Cob, CT
14 Actress Moran
15 Banks and Ford
16 Choose
17 Desk accessory
19 Actor Christopher
20 Sea hawk
21 *Abbie an' Slats* creator Van Buren
23 Burpee products
24 Part of USA
26 Arabian sultanate
27 Goof
28 Eyed
30 Loren's mate
31 Draft org.
32 Hussein's queen
33 Rectories
34 Gloomy
36 Frasier's ex
39 Train storage area
40 Commerce or Treasury: Abbr.
43 Wane
44 Concur
45 Geologic division
46 Llama land
47 Gator cousin
48 Rise up
50 Plains Indian
52 Fill with fizz
53 Boundary: Abbr.
54 *Oktoberfest* entrée
57 Zetterling of *Quartet*
58 Metalsmith
59 Hiker's home
60 Chemical suffix
61 On land __ (everywhere)
62 Betting line

DOWN

1 Takes testimony
2 Pencil ends
3 Little boys
4 Bergen dummy
5 Moist, in a way
6 Metal container?
7 Word form for "one"
8 Cornell team
9 Hungarian composer
10 Spanish direction
11 Op-Ed pieces
12 Run
13 NASA's __ space center
18 Echo
22 Daniel or Pat
24 Ballplayer Matty
25 __-round
29 Barbarian
30 Exploiter
33 Entangle
34 Bit of exercise
35 DEA agent
36 California city
37 Spaniard, e.g.
38 Wyoming city
40 Argued
41 Make believe
42 God-given gifts
44 About
47 Word before letter or mail
49 Poet's Muse
51 Hammett terrier
52 Incantation start
55 Naval rank: Abbr.
56 Dakota Indian

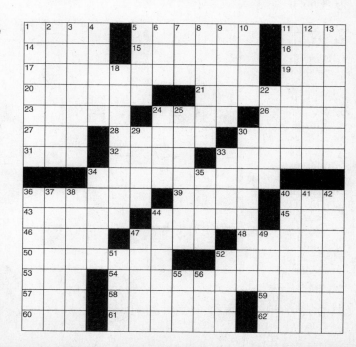

by Frank Longo

ACROSS

1 Mr. Stravinsky
5 Sealing-wax ingredient
8 Paper piece
13 Use a U-Haul
14 Miss. neighbor
15 Actor Everett
16 Haiku, e.g.
17 Cher, to Chastity
18 Kink
19 THEME CLUES
22 Where buoy meets gull
23 Captain's diary
24 Curve shape
25 THEME CLUES
31 Stupefy
32 Preschooler
33 *Exodus* hero
34 Made a choice
37 Chatter
41 Epoch
42 Lend a hand
43 Comedian Philips
44 THEME CLUES
50 Mag execs.
51 Actor Mineo
52 Educators' grp.
53 THE THEME
59 Harsh
60 Calendar abbr.
61 Explorer Heyerdahl
63 Appetite, in psychology
64 CCLI quadrupled
65 Well ventilated
66 Hawk homes
67 SST heading
68 Cape on the Seward Peninsula

DOWN

1 Little pest
2 Mess up
3 Superior to
4 Lax
5 Excoriate
6 Succulent houseplant
7 The Kennedy era
8 Bulgar, e.g.
9 Sharpen
10 City in Wisconsin
11 Join the Navy
12 Microscopic
15 Male deer
20 Get the joke
21 Namath of football
25 Owned
26 Must pay
27 Some genes
28 Coal carrier
29 Buddy
30 Southern constellation
35 Anger
36 Dollop
37 Indy stop
38 Adjusting easily
39 Rhea's look-alike
40 CD follower
42 Martin/Tomlin film
44 Backs at the track
45 Cling
46 Pack animals
47 Install carpeting
48 Ultimate degree
49 Highlander's pattern
54 Teller's cry
55 Cubist painter
56 *Topaz* novelist
57 Mississippi feeder
58 Contemptible person
62 Whole wheat alternative

DOUBLE JEOPARDY

by Eileen Lexau

ACROSS

1 George Ruth
5 Western of '53
10 Scripto rival
13 Roman journey
14 Prestigious prize
15 Sufficient, to Spenser
17 One of a film pair
19 Under control
20 Proof abbr.
21 Bitterly pungent
22 On a cruise
23 Opens
25 Mounts
26 Idyllic place
27 Dorothy's dog
29 Never, in Berlin
30 Belief
33 Algerian port
34 French seasoning
35 Typical situation for 17 Across and 59 Across
40 "Smoking or __?"
41 *Clueless* catchphrase
42 34th Pres.
43 Mao __-tung
44 Keystone __
45 Clothing
49 Waited
51 Flair
54 Adams and others
55 Myanmar's former name
57 Cicero's heart
58 Author Jaffe
59 One of a film pair
61 Litigant
62 Curtain material
63 Gas, e.g.
64 Attempt
65 Goes a round with Foreman
66 Actress Harper

DOWN

1 Cream soup
2 Go to
3 Parish official
4 Sea bird
5 Nosh
6 Office schedule
7 Dugout
8 Have to have
9 Pipe joint
10 Davis or Midler
11 Sort of
12 Some of Shakespeare's plays
16 Equivocators
18 Fond du __, WI
22 Did penance
24 ". . . with a blue ribbon __"
25 Retail booth
27 Dandies
28 Word form for "mouth"
31 Military hats
32 Subatomic particle
35 Pollen holders
36 Barely beat
37 Short gag
38 Actor Torn
39 Big prefix
46 Accumulate
47 Aegean island
48 Emerald and aquamarine
50 Honeybunch
51 Abbey bigwig
52 Agreeing words
53 Slangy denial
55 Radar spot
56 Arm bone
59 Cricket sides
60 To the rear

ACROSS

1 Scruff
5 NYC cultural inst.
9 Pronounce
14 Savings plans
15 Biblical twin
16 Sea eagles
17 Slogan
19 Reds and whites
20 Uses a stylus
21 Fleur-de-__
23 Prime-time hour
24 That girl
25 Door openers
27 Prepared a second draft of
30 Irate
31 Fuss
32 Beloved
34 Leash
38 Social clod
40 Upright
42 Presidents' Day event
43 Likewise
45 Noted naturalist
47 Canterbury can
48 Arrest
50 University of Cincinnati athlete
52 Set of computer commands
56 Japanese drama
57 Part of ABC
58 Service charge
59 Underwater outfits
62 Divided, as a highway
64 '60s game show, with *The*
66 Govt. bill

67 Home to billions
68 Wharton subj.
69 More logical
70 Deion Sanders' nickname
71 Piece of comedy

DOWN

1 Pleasant
2 "I smell __!"
3 Like some quilts
4 Optical illusionist/artist
5 Kitten cries
6 Bolivian bruin
7 Ex-Mrs. Trump
8 IRS work
9 Put in stitches
10 Baubles
11 "Tomorrow" girl
12 Wee
13 Slalom tracks
18 Biblical king
22 Fala was one
25 Regan's dad
26 Charlemagne's realm: Abbr.
27 Punjab princess
28 Perfect place
29 Angry
33 Comment, in computerese
35 Trunkless car
36 Author Kazan
37 Dollars for quarters
39 Unconnected
41 Raise to the third power

44 Unspecified degree
46 Dressing choice
49 Retailer of rhyme
51 Makeup selection
52 Estonians and Latvians
53 RadaRange maker
54 Mortise mate
55 Driver's option
59 Quick read
60 Mine, in Marseilles
61 Posted
63 __ *Spiegel*
65 Uruguayan uncle

79 BAA-BAA

by Bob Lubbers

ACROSS
1 Amoeba, e.g.
5 Way
9 Sp. ladies
13 Mishmash
14 Director Kazan
15 Hokkaido city
16 Thrashed
18 Rising star
19 Electrical unit
20 Lassos
22 "__ De-Lovely"
24 Scythe tracks
26 Bring order to
31 Bargain sign
33 At __ for words
34 Racetrack shapes
36 NT bk.
37 Dull
38 Pitchers
39 Religious image
40 Wager
41 Sidestep
42 Nixon's Secretary of Transportation
43 Guarantee
45 Order
47 On one's back
49 Part of R.S.V.P.
50 Lowest minor league
52 Baked __ (dessert)
57 "__ Whoopee"
59 Stevenson classic
61 Hebrew letters
62 Anthony or Barbara

63 __ off (sore)
64 Impudent
65 Former Haitian president Préval
66 EMK et al.

DOWN
1 Soft drink
2 Actor Jack
3 Sagging
4 Stud site
5 100 centimos
6 Model Carol
7 Layer
8 Mythical underworld
9 Summer ermines
10 Rickety
11 Exist

12 Big __, CA
15 Southern constellation
17 Seed covers
21 MP prey
23 Vermont ski center
25 Sailboats
26 Religious teacher
27 Barkin and Drew
28 European bird
29 Seat, slangily
30 Chris of tennis
32 Ocean fliers
35 *Ars gratia __*
38 Half the digits

39 Charged particle
41 Suffix meaning "believers"
42 Country estate
44 Raise, as spirits
46 Oscar-winner Wiest
48 Sand ridge
51 Helper
53 Urban dwellings: Abbr.
54 *Graf __*
55 Sharp
56 Puts in
57 Chart
58 Hearty brew
60 Playroom

by Dean Niles

ACROSS

1 Auguries
6 Group symbol
12 Hallway
15 Think
16 They come and go
17 Light carriage
18 __ *volente*
19 Bank acct. plus
20 Reporter Batista
21 Icelandic epic
23 Mets' stadium
25 Doubting retort
28 Clairvoyant ability
30 Shoulder muscle, for short
32 Up to spec
33 Asian sheep
35 Took the part
37 Still, in verse
38 Request in advance
40 Shannon's home
42 Lubricate
43 Buckin' pony
45 __ *Angelicus* (Franck work)
46 Folkloric collections
48 Greek meeting place
49 Letters of urgency
50 Scuba gear
51 Part of TAE
53 Two-person fight
56 "Mack the Knife" singer
59 Fade away
61 Superfund org.
62 Of an artery
64 Embroiled
66 Sheep shearing
67 Hit the high points
68 Tucked in
69 Gnats and brats

DOWN

1 Lead source
2 Chevalier song
3 Garden spots
4 Lawrence Welk or Peggy Lee
5 Sp. lady
6 Japanese soup
7 Rub-__
8 Its capital is Belgrade
9 Billy Ocean tune
10 Resident: Suff.
11 Mystery writer Josephine
12 Yield
13 Newspaper page
14 Certain chicken
20 Monopoly square
22 Without delay
24 Common Market inits., once
26 Kate Nelligan role
27 Manages
29 Commoner
31 Word form for "thrice"
33 WWII sub
34 Queen: Sp.
36 *Ed Wood* star
39 __ *longa, vita brevis*
41 *Shane* star
44 Lon of Cambodia
47 Emulated Kerrigan
52 Fosters wrong
54 Pentathlon need
55 Friday's employer: Abbr.
57 Playwright Elmer
58 Chilled
60 Whack
62 Wright-Patterson __, OH
63 __ Miss
64 Keystone comic
65 Belittle, slangily

81 REMEMBERING GENE

by Bob Lubbers

ACROSS

1 Turkish city
6 '70s ring champ
9 Emoter
12 Grows limp
13 Chaney, Sr. or Jr.
14 Pie __ mode
15 Gene Kelly musical of '49
17 Slopes rig
18 Tina's ex
19 Yearn
20 Show gratitude to
21 Some Balkanites
24 Faded star
26 Winter jacket
28 Well-versed
31 Teherani
35 *The Man in the __ Mask*
36 Gene Kelly musical of '52
40 Greek portico
41 Flapjack flipper
42 Arenas
44 Wickerwork material
48 Uncomfortable position
52 Gettysburg general
53 Mexican money
55 Cop a __
57 Carmine or cherry
58 Tsar name
59 Gene Kelly musical of '44
62 Auto
63 General Amin
64 Brouhaha
65 Inquire
66 "__ Cents a Dance"
67 Tennis rankings

DOWN

1 Aroused
2 Moola
3 Computer key
4 High degree
5 Cruising
6 Hail or farewell
7 Rob and Chad
8 Small hotel
9 Cuban dance
10 Alda or Hale
11 Notch
16 "Tut tut!"
17 Gene Kelly musical of '48
18 *The Heart __ Lonely Hunter*
20 __-Mex cuisine
22 Gene Kelly musical of '54
23 Delhi dress
25 Role for Navarro or Heston
27 Dole's state
29 King, in France
30 WWF broadcaster
32 Tang
33 Actress Balin
34 Lwyr.
36 Draft org.
37 Addams' cousin
38 Genesis craft
39 Character actor Jack
43 Part of TGIF
45 Punished severely
46 Fred's sister et al.
47 Actor Beatty
49 Lyric poem
50 Sergeant York
51 Shirt shape
53 12-point type
54 Gabor and Perón
56 Weaponry
59 Op. __ (footnote tag)
60 "Golly!"
61 __ du Diable

82 WATER LOG

by Gregory E. Paul

ACROSS

1 Embarrass
6 Smelter leftover
10 Sci-fi creature
14 Ma's instrument
15 Flooring unit
16 Berg opera
17 Evil spirit
18 Ugandan dictator
19 PC operator
20 National park
22 A James Bond school
23 Comprehend
24 Satan's doing
26 Cable network
31 Mideast VIP
35 New York college
36 Dozes off
38 Playing marble
39 Marathoner Zátopek
40 Subway stations
42 Buck heroine
43 Crystal-lined stone
45 Kovacs' wife
46 '52 Olympics site
47 Opry star Tubb
49 Casey Jones, e.g.
51 Tooth's partner
53 *Platoon* locale
54 Dance pattern
57 Jefferson Memorial sight
63 Mississippi feeder
64 Berserk
65 "__ It Through the Rain"
66 Flowerless plant
67 Midevening
68 Activist Abzug
69 Prepared to drive
70 Phone key
71 Computer key

DOWN

1 Like some appliances
2 Suds
3 __ mater
4 Letter drop
5 "No fooling!"
6 Deadlock
7 Succotash bean
8 Similarly
9 Convention city
10 Brooke Shields film, with *The*
11 A deadly sin
12 Grocery buy
13 Be angry
21 Tack-room gear
25 Savings plan, for short
26 Long onslaught
27 Round-tripper
28 Salad add-in
29 "Life in the Woods" locale
30 Horace work
32 Quiz choice
33 Dickens title start
34 Pavarotti, e.g.
37 Regatta sight
41 *Love Story* author
44 Spanish pronoun
48 Giants
50 Drink
52 The sky, perhaps
54 Cushy
55 Quaker pronoun
56 Shamrock isle
58 Lisbon lady
59 Revival shout
60 NaCl
61 Run in place
62 At hand

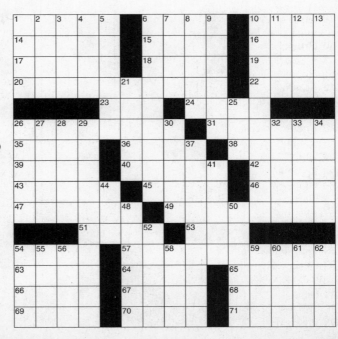

83 HOW MANY MOVIES?

by Bob Lubbers

ACROSS
1 Latin dance
6 Sap producer
11 Bruins hero
14 Spin
15 Ring source?
16 Corp. boss
17 Davis/Baxter film of '50
19 Swelled head
20 Shore
21 Dart
22 Gibson or Tillis
25 Aliens, for short
26 Veiled dancer
28 Stage cue
30 Beef or veal
33 In a while
34 Scanty
36 Peres predecessor
38 Sinatra/Martin film of '58
43 Senator Specter
44 Tributary
45 Classic violin
48 Urchin
50 "Whatever __ wants, . . ."
51 Scale start
53 Satire mag
55 Law deg.
56 Barnum singer
57 Singer Cole
61 Anger
62 Cruise/ Nicholson film of '92
66 __-relief
67 Weird
68 Gorby's late wife
69 Draft org.
70 Croakers
71 Shatter

DOWN
1 RR depot
2 Hole maker
3 Wire measure
4 Bikini tops
5 *Three Tall Women* playwright
6 Fluffy dessert
7 Against
8 Like a noted piper
9 Adores
10 Chemical suffix
11 Spotted cat
12 Government
13 Fan
18 Breakfast choice
21 Napped fabric
22 GI dining room
23 National Leaguer
24 Actor Neeson
27 True up
29 Paid the tab
31 Fight site
32 Sailor
35 Theater drop
37 City near Niagara Falls
39 Small gull
40 Role model, perhaps
41 Singer Carter
42 Alum
45 Improvs
46 Shearer and Kelly
47 *The Thing* star
49 Reflections
52 Surmise
54 Certain fashions
58 Nautical start
59 Tree shoot
60 Waxed cheese
62 Gen. Pershing's command
63 Farrow or Sara
64 Road curve
65 Slangy turndown

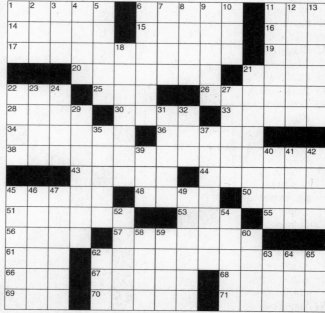

WHO'S COOKIN'

by Dean Niles

ACROSS

1. Blind as __
5. __ *Buddies* (Hanks sitcom)
10. Hideout
14. Biblical verb
15. 50 Across' métier
16. Otherwise
17. *American Cookery* author
19. __ monster
20. Commences
21. Not for kids
23. Cereal sound
24. State formed in 1948
27. *Art of Cooking* author
32. XLV x X
35. Troubled
36. "Smooth Operator" singer
37. Commotion
39. Fuel choice
41. Cleveland's lake
42. 2000 candidate
45. Gal of song
46. *Boston Cooking School Cookbook* author
50. Soprano Maria
51. Promontory
54. Narrow passages
57. Genie's specialty
59. New York stadium
60. *Mastering the Art of French Cooking* author
64. Daybreak
65. Out and about
66. __ *la Douce*
67. *M*A*S*H* star
68. Baseball great Wagner
69. Pinnacle

DOWN

1. Pts. of speech
2. Cats and canoes
3. The self, in Hinduism
4. British rule in India
5. Hope and Hoskins
6. Uncover, to Keats
7. Big wave
8. Bobby of hockey
9. Colorful weave
10. Brief words
11. Disembarked
12. Gilligan's home
13. Interpret
18. Saul, latterly
22. Salesperson
24. Smarts stats
25. Bring to court
26. Like Sen. Dole
28. Number-cruncher: Abbr.
29. Skip a bid
30. Brainstorm
31. Role for Jodie
32. Kitchen boss
33. Copperfield's first wife
34. Steak cut
38. Liking
39. DC party
40. Peaceful
42. Pro sports org.
43. Top bond rating
44. AMA members
47. "__ Woman" (Reddy tune)
48. Biblical prophet
49. Send again
52. English county
53. City in the news in '65
54. Beliefs
55. Exhibit
56. Hatcher or Garr
57. 800-no. rel.
58. Wyo. neighbor
61. USAF headache
62. Screen Chaney
63. Marker

85 SWEET STUFF

by Thomas W. Schier

ACROSS
1 Actor Lee J.
5 __ B'rith
9 Notices
13 Atmosphere
14 Start again
15 Pressed (on)
17 Facial ridge
18 Director Reitman
19 Homeric enchantress
20 Candy-shop selections
23 Interject
25 Antediluvian
26 Put together snugly
27 Candy-shop selections
31 Relig. title
32 Take __ (accept risk)
33 Humid
35 Comic Martha
36 Mischievous one
38 Pancake place, initially
42 Former German coin
44 First-century pope
45 Male swan
48 Candy-shop selection
51 Burdens
53 Cable channel
54 Wind dir.
55 Candy-shop selection
59 Clayey
60 Lopez's theme song
61 Matured

64 __ a customer
65 Sign to heed
66 Shoreline recess
67 One-pot meal
68 Split violently
69 Author Wister

DOWN
1 Urban vehicle
2 Sharers' word
3 Cohan's favorite address
4 Cry loudly
5 Pull in
6 The Silver State
7 __ at the Races
8 Charged atoms

9 Achievement
10 Satie and Estrada
11 Marsh birds
12 Hush-hush
16 Since: Sp.
21 Folk tales
22 Tear open
23 Open a bit
24 Baby's word
28 Pitcher Saberhagen
29 Sears rival
30 Around the 30th: Abbr.
34 Wedding-cake feature
36 Move through mud
37 Bus. mogul
39 Slammer

40 Fixes a squeak
41 Carpet asset
43 Was shown up
44 "I __ Song Go . . ."
45 Jazz group
46 Burger toppers
47 Roy Rogers' dog
49 Like some bases
50 Away from the sea
52 Rollerblade
56 __ close to schedule
57 Attend, with "to"
58 Folded food
62 Actress Arden
63 Lair

by Bob Lubbers

ACROSS

1 Jazzy Washington
6 Satiate
10 Einstein colleague
14 Actress Verdugo
15 Tops
16 __ vera
17 Protest tactic
18 Affable fellow
20 Held onto
21 Bolted
22 Vistas
23 __ avis
25 Confuse
26 Chou's comrade
28 "Ho-hum!"
33 TV alien
34 Norway export
35 USC stats
39 Persevere
42 Oz dog
43 Idle
44 King's employer
45 Soaped up
47 WBA wins
48 Mortar worker
51 __ spumante
53 "__ Fideles"
55 Hockey Hall-of-Famer
57 "__ it rich?"
60 Boxer Walcott
62 Detest
63 Olympian Korbut
64 Citrus skin
65 Rostropovich's instrument
66 Stagger
67 "Zounds!"
68 Use a fitting room

DOWN

1 Rolltop, e.g.
2 Tennis pro Nastase
3 Annual-report stat
4 O'Day or Loos
5 Solo of *Star Wars*
6 Loopy
7 Lake diver
8 Numero __
9 Danson and Knight
10 Shirred item
11 Chan portrayer
12 Hailey bestseller
13 Della or Pee Wee
19 Lasting impression
21 Drumroll
24 Hazard
26 Sail support
27 Sax range
29 Indolence
30 Dean Martin song topic
31 Gaffe
32 Bend __ (talk too much)
36 In a mischievous manner
37 __ domini
38 Retirees' IDs
40 Huge
41 Norms: Abbr.
46 Chip in
48 Important
49 Designer Simpson
50 Lint collector
52 Rome's river
54 *Jane* __
55 Wife of Charlie Chaplin
56 Funny Foxx
58 __ contendere
59 Disney sci-fi film
61 Lively dance
62 False front

87 OUTSIDE THE LAW

by Diane C. Baldwin

ACROSS
1 Monica of tennis
6 Barber's need
11 Chew the fat
14 Drab hue
15 Deb's crown
16 Time to remember
17 Papillon was one
19 Take first
20 Real lulu
21 Sommer of *The Prize*
22 Jacket material
24 Horsehair
26 Fishhook attachments
27 Ornate style
30 Least vivid
32 Midwest airport
33 Shady recess
34 Bricklayer's tote
37 Location
38 Winter weather
39 Pitchfork poker
40 Whimper
41 Eat well
42 Musical selection
43 Hedger's word
45 Norman or Faldo
46 Tremulous
48 Peacock's pride
49 Easy to tote
50 Boot attachment
52 Verdi masterpiece
56 Feeling off
57 Cat Ballou was one
60 Pie __ mode
61 Old $10 gold coin

62 Smart __ (wise guy)
63 Neighbor of Isr.
64 Transactions
65 President Bush's state

DOWN
1 Just fair
2 Zest
3 Photo magazine
4 Henceforth
5 Wine-bottle word
6 Old hat
7 Sound of time passing
8 Leaf gatherer
9 Bonanza find
10 Ginger, to Fred

11 The Lone Wolf was one
12 Shakespearean sprite
13 Wizards' sticks
18 Town near Tahoe
23 Hoopster Unseld
25 Flying wonder
26 Pigeonhole
27 Clooney, on *ER*
28 Part of B&O
29 Hudson Hawk was one
30 Fourth Estate
31 Aid a criminal
33 "Ah me!"
35 In the past
36 Antelope's playmate?

38 Kernel
39 Fit for cultivation
41 Moved like a moth
42 Luau food
44 "Nope"
45 Teri of *Tootsie*
46 Felonious handle
47 Future mare
48 Melodies
50 Epic tale
51 Vitamin medium
53 Wild goat
54 Word form for "ten"
55 Torah holders
58 Actress __ Dawn Chong
59 Feedbag bit

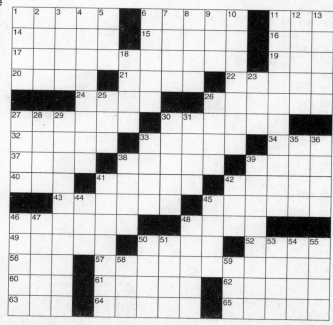

by Dean Niles

ACROSS

1 Breakfast order
5 Basketball player
10 Summer shirts
14 Steak order
15 As __ (usually)
16 Author O'Brien
17 Oil cartel
18 Kind of bug
19 Part of QED
20 Bubble up
22 Wildebeest
23 The Bruins: Abbr.
24 Bird beak
25 Most out of shape
27 Kit's partner
30 Diamond __
31 Tolstoy's Ilyich
32 Dawn goddess
33 Source of the Mississippi
37 Spasm
38 Little pest
39 Winter hazard
40 Dutch uncle
41 Nanook was one
43 "Put __ Happy Face"
44 Peak
45 White House advisory grp.
46 Starter
48 Rural music
52 Tenn. neighbor
53 *The __ of Spring*
54 Circle part
55 Some T-shirts
58 Persian poet
59 Needle
61 Thailand, once
62 Biblical visitors
63 Hidden
64 Spanish compass point
65 Halt
66 Brahman, e.g.
67 Lamb dish

DOWN

1 Cupid's equivalent
2 Look amazed
3 Party founded in 1874
4 Slice
5 Gumshoe's job
6 Dance or drama
7 Water sounds
8 Actress Verdugo
9 Party founded in 1854
10 Bar order
11 Draw forth
12 Hydroxyl compounds
13 Camp David Accords signatory
21 Cinemax rival
25 Lay an egg
26 Small taste
27 Give as an example
28 Alamo rival
29 Party founded in 1828
34 Party founded in 1901
35 Crooner Perry
36 Pews response
38 "__ Excited" (Pointer Sisters song)
39 1953 Pulitzer playwright
42 Meantime
43 Lubricant holders
44 Graphic references
47 "__ the Walrus"
48 Seniors' events
49 Get in one's sights
50 Put on
51 Field of competition
55 Desiccated
56 Recent
57 Eurasian duck
60 Game, __, match

by Dean Niles

ACROSS

1 Victuals
5 Golfer Ballesteros
9 Pauley of NBC
13 Caribbean resort
14 Sooner city
15 Draft animals
16 Arrives
17 Fairy
18 __ *Three Lives*
19 They're paper-trained
22 Massage area
23 River arm
24 World-carrying figure
28 __ d'oeuvres
29 Authorized
31 "Do __ say . . ."
32 Long-haired cat
35 Compass dir.
36 Some sandwiches
37 Kiddie-lit characters
40 Was indebted to
41 Crude, for one
42 Land of Grieg
43 Colorado Indian
44 Shade source
45 Origin
46 Copier need
48 __ Cologne
50 *Juin* predecessor
53 Dan Haggerty TV role
56 Like some floors
59 "Body and __ "
60 Bedding
61 Surmounting
62 Pertaining to
63 "__ Wanna Cry" (Mariah Carey song)
64 Body of a book
65 Start a lawn
66 Transgressions

DOWN

1 Collection
2 Cuban dance
3 Above, in Berlin
4 Of humble parentage
5 Indian soldiers
6 *Diciembre* successor
7 Horowitz, Rubinstein, et al.
8 Peter Gunn's girlfriend
9 Reinforcing beam
10 Rocker Rose
11 Born, in Brest
12 Goal
13 S&L units
20 Shade source
21 Energy dose
25 Former NBC series
26 *Ad __ per aspera*
27 Mama's boy
28 Gardened, maybe
30 Big name in Massachusetts
32 Roughly
33 __ the neighborhood (just moved in)
34 Inexperienced
35 Gal of song
36 Roadshoulder
38 Longitudinal division
39 Aurora __
44 Blow it
45 Hoodwinked
47 Land of Thebes
49 Cerulean
50 Massenet opera
51 Agreements, in church
52 "Small world, __ it?"
54 Egyptian goddess
55 Actress Conn
56 Angkor __
57 Broke bread
58 Tic-tac-toe loser

90 SAY IT AGAIN

by Matt Gaffney

ACROSS

1 Roseanne, née __
5 Mediterranean port
9 Land ending
14 "Aha!"
15 Prom wheels
16 Passageways
17 City on the Dnieper
18 Take __ (acknowledge applause)
19 Ahead
20 Theater category
23 Pantsmaker Strauss
24 Hosiery shade
25 Immature insect
28 Hot drink
30 Doctors' grp.
33 Least friendly
35 Defendants: Lat.
36 Pierce
37 Literary genre
40 Kitchen sight
41 Dearie
42 Zodiac sign
43 Morse plea
44 Unauthorized TV greeting
46 Stares at
47 Roll reply
48 North Carolina college
50 Family tree member
56 Panache
57 Diving birds
58 Quaker pronoun
59 Singing cowboy
60 Lose solidity
61 Forever and a day
62 '50s Dodger shortstop
63 Ben & Jerry's rival
64 Ladies

DOWN

1 Denzel Washington role
2 *Clueless* cry
3 Surfing hazard
4 Some arms
5 Former king of Norway
6 Frog sound
7 *Omnia vincit* __
8 "That's logical!"
9 Poorly made
10 "__ talk?": Rivers
11 Utah resort
12 Maneuver
13 Clairvoyant's claim
21 Famine alternative
22 Checks
25 Talks like Cindy Brady
26 Ragweed reaction
27 They're hysterical
29 Maine town
30 Eniwetok, e.g.
31 Runner Sydney
32 Bottomless pit
34 *Grease* garb
36 Makes no progress
38 What the Maple Leafs play in Toronto
39 "Move it!"
44 Crier's cry
45 With deference
47 Legacy recipients
49 Cobbler's forms
50 Stamp feature
51 Have standing
52 Regretted
53 Fulghum book
54 Hawaiian bird
55 Hardy heroine
56 Nowhere near

91 LOW-RENT DISTRICT

by Gregory E. Paul

ACROSS

1 *"O __ Mio"*
5 With 29 Across, jazz pianist
10 Study hard
14 High-school dance
15 Emergency signal
16 Lunar light
17 Pent-up problem
19 Scent
20 Brown brew
21 On the briny
22 Egg stone
24 Odyssey
25 __-Christian ethic
26 Find not guilty
29 See 5 Across
32 Bind (up)
33 *The Price Is Right* shout
34 Cry's partner
35 Glimpse
36 Propelled a gondola
37 Kismet
38 New England cape
39 Folklore being
40 Transparent
41 Conferences
43 Curious George is one
44 "We have met the __ . . ."
45 A gift of the Magi
46 Zen goal
48 Quasimodo's charge
49 Actress Zetterling
52 *Cinco + tres*
53 Hooverville
56 Bible bk.
57 Banks of the Cubs
58 Weirdo
59 Part of D.A.
60 Luster
61 Yet

DOWN

1 Humane org.
2 Ph.D. exam
3 Ear part
4 British record label
5 Counterbalance
6 Glossy
7 Vena __
8 Exist
9 Sent another way
10 Anger
11 Electronics chain
12 Gobs
13 *Utopia* author
18 Nostril
23 Baltic Sea feeder
24 Walrus feature
25 Sparkler
26 Mythical Titan
27 Witch
28 Marine's dwelling
29 Surveys
30 Navel type
31 Impecunious
33 Bonkers
36 Takes an oath
37 The "F" in UNICEF
39 Layer
40 Sucker, for short
42 Snobbish
43 Liquefied
45 Wish granter
46 Drink mixer
47 Word form for "vinegar"
48 Scourge
49 Apollo goal
50 Leatherneck on the lam
51 Black
54 Buckingham initials
55 Ring result: Abbr.

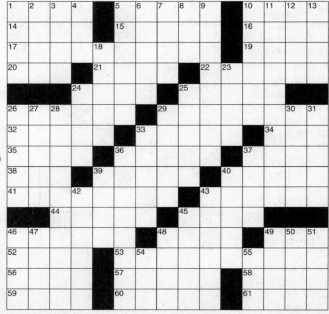

TOWNIES

by Bob Lubbers

ACROSS

1 Bottom lines?
5 Bronze and Iron
9 Shiny minerals
14 Mayberry lad
15 Domesticated
16 Texas mission
17 Sup
18 Fedora feature
19 Girls: Sp.
20 English urbanites
23 *Ben-__*
24 Skater Midori
25 Firstborn
27 Builds
29 Theda of the silents
31 Classic car
32 Flashy fish
33 Reporter Ernie
34 Beginner
35 California urbanites
38 Extremity
41 Regretful sound
42 Key letter
46 "This __ raid!"
47 Burn inside
48 Hardly ever
49 Pancake ingredient
51 Alley of the funnies
52 A Bobbsey twin
53 English urbanites
57 Country estate
58 Sailing
59 Drink garnish
61 Mug
62 Soon
63 Eye drop
64 Sows
65 See 45 Down
66 Greek peak

DOWN

1 Brick carrier
2 Gourmet
3 Mosque tower
4 Espied
5 Diamond statistics
6 Enigmatic star
7 Desert chieftain
8 Truck rig
9 Type of paper
10 Homeric epic
11 Tuna packager
12 Fortune builder
13 "Mayday!"
21 Giant
22 Bridge maven Charles
23 __ up (excited)
26 Also
28 Sole stuffing
29 Club rule
30 Pub draws
33 Soccer great
34 Despot
36 Florida athlete
37 Giraffe cousin
38 Sass
39 Set apart
40 Afternoon performance
43 Cents
44 Blood components
45 With 65 Across, *The Fountainhead* author
47 Boat ends
48 Actor Young of *Topper*
50 Shun
51 Greek theater
54 Carson followed him
55 Pres. Carter's alma mater
56 Marian Anderson, e.g.
57 Editors' concerns: Abbr.
60 Time to remember

93 LIQUIDITY

by Rich Norris

ACROSS

1 Small particles
6 Therefore
10 Locking device
14 Easygoing gaits
15 Cookout unit
16 Jazzy James
17 Can't be substantiated
20 Gumbo ingredient
21 Bar for a team
22 Listing
23 CEO's PDQ
25 Film connections
27 Gallic witticism
29 Essential part
32 Dusk, to Donne
33 Out on __ (at risk)
35 Like some causes
37 F followers
41 Accelerate
44 Midmonth date
45 Table d'__
46 Made a choice
47 Restorative retreat
49 That woman's
51 Word form for "three"
52 Leak preventers
56 "Oops!"
58 "And we'll have __ good time"
59 Prof. rank
62 Tub parts, at times
65 Faces reality
68 Hard work
69 Nocturnal noise
70 Transactions
71 Sea swoopers
72 Ceases
73 Artist Max

DOWN

1 *Battle Cry* actor Ray
2 Made off with
3 Spy
4 Monument Valley sights
5 Payroll ID no.
6 Bounce back
7 Castle, in chess
8 Beaufort-scale entries
9 Overused, as a joke
10 Intensifying
11 Top story
12 Inscribed stone
13 Labor associate?
18 Kind
19 Fabric texture
24 Prefix for valence
26 Tennis star Sampras
27 Ancient traveling trio
28 Fetid
30 Furthermore
31 Nail's partner
34 Service cafeterias
36 Hook's helper
38 Became troublesome
39 Bakery worker
40 Skywalker was one
42 Where she blows
43 Kid
48 __-mell
50 Campus recruiter: Abbr.
52 Fritter away
53 Knight clothes
54 Welcome, as to one's home
55 Squelched
57 Propose
60 Wearing loafers, perhaps
61 Preps a table
63 Moray and conger
64 Try out
66 That girl
67 Praiseful poem

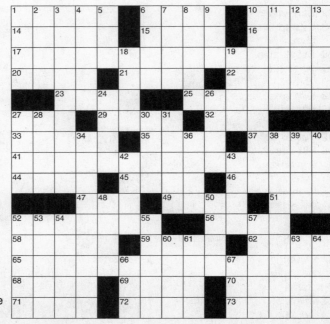

DOUBLESPEAK

by Frank Longo

ACROSS

1 *Masquerade* actor
5 Toolhouse
9 Throw out a line
13 "__ we all?"
15 Shudder at
16 Chinese gelatin
17 Have good penmanship
19 Food fish
20 Rut
21 Tori's dad
22 Flu symptom
24 Outlawed combo
27 Perpetually
29 Yachting
30 Conductor from India
31 Parting words
33 Wood cutter
36 Afore
37 Bangkok haberdashery item
40 Greek letter
41 *Guys & Dolls* name
42 Like some pizza
43 Pass out
45 Ball-__ hammer
47 Punishing rod
48 Plunder a construction site
53 Right-angled extensions
54 Snide remark
55 Camels' cousins
57 Peril
58 Collection of stems
62 Olympic weapon
63 Hors d'oeuvre offering
64 U.S. air-base site in Greenland
65 Shoe strip
66 Mid-sermon interjection
67 Paste

DOWN

1 Bill's future
2 Big-name Bruin
3 Do a dairy job
4 Beg
5 Hindu Trinity member
6 Golf great Walter
7 Neighbor of Som.
8 *NYPD Blue* role
9 Honeydew's relative
10 Forum's Greek counterpart
11 Styling site
12 Vogue
14 Jazzman Macero
18 Sticks up
21 20th-century fabulist
22 *Zapped!* star
23 Record keeper
25 Decked out
26 Actor Morales
28 Sun __-sen
31 Befoul
32 Experience malaise
33 Korean
34 Bikini, for one
35 Lets up
38 Ground breakers
39 Language ending
44 Holiday hangups
45 Mail-carrying vessel
46 Shoe leather
47 Criticism
48 Wood holder
49 Rubbish
50 Studio stand
51 Delight
52 Comic DeGeneres
56 Wyo. setting
58 Steamroom site
59 Hebrides headgear
60 Actor Gulager
61 Beer barrel

95 HAVE A HEARTH

by Lee Weaver

ACROSS

1 Shade trees
5 Make a trade
9 Oddly amusing
14 Money in Teheran
15 *Murphy Brown* barkeep
16 Dashboard device
17 European volcano
18 Long lunch?
19 All thumbs
20 Flue dweller
23 Movie ad
24 Bar crawler
25 AWOL's nemeses
28 Shed tears
31 Singer Brewer
33 Pile up
37 Math-table number
39 The __ Ranger
40 The sun
41 Prepare for a test
42 Gambler's expression
45 Attracting attention
46 Mother's little __
47 Jalopy
49 Lemony quaff
50 Society newcomer
52 Least polite
57 Kitchen device
60 Cowboy contest
63 Alluring
64 Fishline adjunct
65 Write, in a way
66 Vocal
67 Add fringe to
68 Encounters
69 Docile
70 Gardener's purchase

DOWN

1 Straight up
2 Supple
3 Excessive enthusiasm
4 Bridge coups
5 Field of knowledge
6 Miss Muffet's fare
7 Affected mannerisms
8 Farm tools
9 Itinerant
10 Carry on
11 Praiseful poem
12 Golf-hole edge
13 Sodom survivor
21 Fresh information
22 Small amount
25 Montréal's subway
26 Old exclamation
27 Davis or Kaye
29 Famous lioness
30 Asta, for one
32 Well-heeled
33 __ and omega
34 Lowed
35 Place for a bracelet
36 Trickle
38 High spirits
43 Frankfurters
44 Unfettered
45 Sharp projection
48 Sock pattern
51 Infatuate
53 Valleys
54 Piano practice piece
55 Suit fabric
56 Cornered
57 Indian head, e.g.
58 Blood components
59 Final, for one
60 Tach letters
61 Assay specimen
62 Engraved stamp

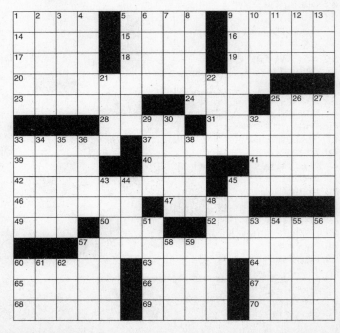

96 TWO-FOR-ONE

by Wayne Robert Williams

ACROSS

1 Fury
5 Calculating rack
11 Cohort of Fidel
14 Runner Zátopek
15 Turkey part
16 Little shaver
17 First name in crooning
18 Beach Boys song
20 Wong of *The Thief of Bagdad*
22 Fine meal
23 S&L offering
24 Mound stat.
27 Writer Rombauer and others
28 Bauxite or pyrite
30 Sponge cake
33 Frolicked
35 Attention
36 Delay
40 Employee at the first tee
42 Fidgety
44 Butter alternative
45 Peggy or Spike
47 Thin material
48 *Dallas* role
51 Concert box
52 Post fresh troops
55 Port St. Lucie's locale
56 Beloved person
58 Is of use
60 Daughter of Tommy Chong
64 Writer Oates
67 *"Dies __"*
68 Blotter initials
69 Superlatively achy
70 Wear out
71 Guys
72 Cornerstone tablets
73 Post

DOWN

1 Big name in country
2 Former African despot
3 Federal mortgage agency
4 "Pomp and Circumstance" composer
5 "Fernando" group
6 Ink roller
7 Gas: Pref.
8 Truck compartment
9 Mil. branch
10 Botanist's line
11 Assertion
12 Barbera's partner
13 Best and O'Brien
19 Transfixes
21 *American Buffalo* dramatist
25 White alternative
26 Open a bit
28 Approximately
29 Muslim weight
31 Designer Simpson
32 Rocky ridge
34 Matter-of-fact
37 Celebrated bride of 1994
38 Specialized cell
39 Cry
41 Angler's mecca
43 Burn the end of
46 Building branch
49 Except
50 Singer Julius
52 Hindu title
53 Call to mind
54 Chichén Itzá residents
57 Film cuts
59 Highlander
61 *"Der __"* (Adenauer)
62 Put on guard
63 Yearn for
65 Exist
66 Fam. member

97 ALLITERATES

by Frank Longo

ACROSS
1 Roman date
5 Newswoman Elizabeth
11 Propel a shot
14 Think (over)
15 Asimov et al.
16 *Peer Gynt* character
17 *The Fabulous Baker Boys* star
19 Campaigned
20 Extreme
21 Ending for court or cash
22 Plummer role
23 U-turn from WNW
24 Three-time Wimbledon winner
28 Icicle site
29 Meet a raise
30 Ireland
33 Actress Thurman
35 Astaire's sister
38 *Billy Budd* composer
42 Tie types
43 Magnon lead-in
44 Spanish compass point
45 River island
46 Blues singer James
48 1992 Sullivan Award winner
53 Sine __ non
56 Units of absorbed dose
57 Chou En-__
58 Parts of speech
60 Resident's suffix

61 *Caveman* costar
64 German article
65 San __, TX
66 Maui, for one
67 Dangerous curve
68 Antarctic penguin
69 Cows and ewes

DOWN
1 Saturate
2 Swordfights
3 Make happy
4 Musical marking
5 Man: Lat.
6 "I Wonder __ Wander"
7 Forearm bones

8 Plum varieties
9 Bitter-tasting
10 Conscription org.
11 Talking pets
12 Customary practice
13 Choir member
18 See 62 Down
22 Summer cooler
25 Egg cell
26 Do-fa linkup
27 Actor Morales
28 Commands
30 Retrocede
31 __ Speedwagon
32 Kansans, e.g.
34 Mandela grp.
36 Give the go-ahead
37 Chemical ending

39 Italian wine center
40 La __ Tar Pits
41 French roast
47 Amino acid carrier, for short
48 Shower honoree
49 Hall's partner
50 Spiral-horned antelope
51 Flat boat
52 Defame in print
53 Put down
54 Cry of defeat
55 Fire remnants
59 Kimono sashes
61 Goat's note
62 With 18 Down, *Arabian Nights* persona
63 Salmon-to-be

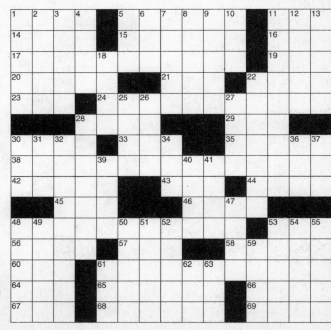

98 DE-LIGHTFUL

by Dean Niles

ACROSS

1 The bad guys
5 Coop group
9 Friar's superior
14 __ facto
15 Angry
16 Grassy expanse
17 Trendy flier
19 Knight weapon
20 I as in Innsbruck
21 __ Tae Woo
22 Paved, in a way
24 "__ in the bud!"
26 Reaction to a rat
27 Without artifice
30 Goalpost part
34 Rolex rivals
36 "Telephone Line" group
37 Kind of sch.
39 Frosh, next year
40 More competent
42 Rhine feeder
43 Clubs, for instance
44 __ Abner
45 Role for Whitmore or Oldman
47 Russian mystic
50 Expiate
51 In fashion
52 Serta competitor
54 Flippered mammal
58 Egyptian cobra
59 __ Mahal
62 Organic compound
63 Unexpected winner
66 Bedding
67 Commedia dell'__
68 Coral formation
69 Slightest
70 Catty comment
71 Unheeding

DOWN

1 South Pacific island group
2 Oil cartel
3 OT book
4 "__ your old man!"
5 Legally curtail
6 Cathedral style
7 Coll. test
8 Certain Slav
9 WWII winners
10 Anna Sewell novel
11 River border
12 Fairy-tale beginning
13 Three-__ sloth
18 Author Jong
23 Tahoe digs
24 Plant family
25 Latticework
27 One in charge
28 Hiroshima, Mon __
29 Photo tint
31 Tijuana cry
32 San Antonio mission
33 Watched the video again
35 Respectful gesture
38 Biblical wall word
41 Bridle piece
46 Mr. Kramden
48 Mighty
49 Close by
53 Crooked
54 Teen hangout
55 Amiens girlfriend
56 Designer Ricci
57 Round cheese
59 Balsam or birch
60 On the bounding main
61 Actor Goldblum
64 "__ we having fun yet?"
65 Former CA fort

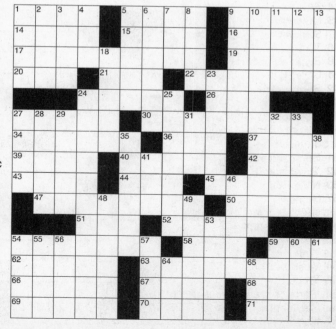

ACROSS

1 Church seating
5 War photographer Robert
9 *Camille* star
14 Kindergarten thru 12th, briefly
15 Arabic letter
16 "Farewell!"
17 Without __ to stand on
18 Volunteer of 1898
20 View point?
22 Cyclists' gear
23 Media outlets
24 Madras wrap
25 Almost
33 Shack
34 Sauce brand
35 Nobelist Soyinka
36 The A. in B.A.
38 Evade
41 Court order
42 Sgts., e.g.
43 Purina rival
45 Mauna __
46 '80s TV drama
51 Endless times
52 '20s auto
53 Noted tenor
57 Sounded like sleigh bells
61 Brit's carousel
63 Country in West Africa
64 Varnish resin
65 Brew: Ger.
66 Revered figure
67 Exposed

68 Cravings
69 __ *kleine Nachtmusik*

DOWN

1 Top level
2 *Vogue* competitor
3 Curds and __
4 Tourist stops
5 New Mexico caverns site
6 Lotion ingredient
7 More: Mus.
8 Colorful blanket
9 Vampire deterrent
10 Take __ view of
11 Astronaut Sally
12 Red vegetable
13 *Yours, Mine and* __
19 Dagwood sandwich
21 Done with
24 Small apartments
25 Intone
26 Stagger
27 "Great" emperor
28 Actor Tognazzi
29 Wobblies' union: Abbr.
30 Author Maxim
31 Foreigner
32 Label again
37 The Ukraine, once: Abbr.
39 Leg
40 Retiree's title

44 Submachine gun
47 Watched over
48 Body-mind system
49 Highfalutin
50 Thwart, in a way
53 Colorless
54 Chaplin's wife
55 Naturalist John
56 "I've Got the Music __"
57 Evita's husband
58 Venues
59 Painter Schiele
60 Finished
62 Mine find

HERE TODAY . . .

by Wayne Robert Williams

ACROSS

1 Reindeer herder
5 Lacking
8 Teamster
14 Switch ender
15 Garden sphere
16 Reduced
17 "Wait a minute!"
18 March of '50s TV
19 Shrinks involuntarily
20 September birthstones
23 Reddish purple
24 Intimidate
25 Spanish aunt
27 Bottom line
28 Dumbstruck state
30 Range-hood elements
33 Ness and Lomond
35 Spotter
36 Deep black
37 Author of *Them*
39 List-ending abbr.
43 "Thanks, Jacques"
45 Paris river
46 Wastrel
51 Recycled T-shirt
52 Monkey suit
53 Peer Gynt's mother
54 Surfeited
56 Seed coverings
58 Gutter's outflow
62 Strip of wood
64 U-turn from WSW

65 Spoken
66 French students
67 German article
68 Gear teeth
69 Passover repasts
70 Liquid qty.
71 Baby bouncer

DOWN

1 Take away
2 Greek river
3 Part of a ship
4 Daddy
5 Enigmatic person
6 Home, figuratively
7 Noted drama school

8 "In what way?"
9 Bring to life
10 Annapolis sch.
11 Hiatus
12 Gridiron complement
13 Changes the timer
21 Shades
22 Knucklehead
26 Osiris' wife
28 Arabic name
29 Avoided defeat
31 Up and about
32 Liberate
34 Choir selection
37 Table scraps
38 Rued the aerobics
40 Tool in a trunk

41 Santa ___, CA
42 Part of a tour
44 *Lou Grant* star
45 Getz or Kenton
46 Balanced conditions
47 Royal shade
48 Told never to come back
49 Spanish composer
50 Leaflets
55 Author/pediatrician
57 Not prerecorded
59 Change completely
60 Beep
61 Otherwise
63 Double curve

1

```
CPAS SWEEP CALF
HOLE CRAZE OREL
IOTA RESIN LOMA
CHARLESTON OMAR
    OAT AERATE
TOMTOM PENN
AROOM JITTERBUG
LEON POLOS HONE
COTILLION DELTA
    PANT ORATOR
ABSENT ODA
LOON TURKEYTROT
TOUT ETUIS OILY
ENSE RALES SLIP
REAR SHESA SLOE
```

2

```
BAKE MARIO SLAP
ALES ORONO HOPE
SALESPITCH AGES
IMP EPOCH APART
COYOTES WOMEN
   THROWOUT STA
SLAT ERRS ROW
POCO MAIMS FUEL
AVE TELL ENDS
NEO WALLSAFE
    FLITE ATALOSS
ALBAN GABON ZAP
BOAR COMINGHOME
BASK IRENE ANON
ADES DYNES MEAD
```

3

```
GRIN SLAIN JAZZ
LODE WORSE OBOE
ABOWLOFCHERRIES
DESSERTS EGEST
    WADS JUNE
LEMONS HERE WPA
ALAMO SATE CHER
BUTANEMPTYDREAM
EDEN COPY RILLE
LED COTY SIMPER
    ZANE DAVE
INALL LIVEWIRE
BOXOFCHOCOLATES
IGOT AUGER VENT
SONY PRODS EMTS
```

4

```
HADAT HOLM TAPE
ARUBA AREA ERIE
RISEN LEAR RILE
MET GREASYNEALE
    YALE DELOS
TABLETS ANADEM
ROALD HORNE ILO
ARKY HEROD FRAT
STE DADDY DITTO
HARPER SPRAYER
    ANDES OATH
MUDDYWATERS AKA
ONER ASIA TURIN
NILE RENT INRED
OTIS ELKS COYLY
```

5

```
ALOAD CASTS POP
LASSO OSSIE ACE
BISHOPSHEEN RUT
    RITE AISLE
RADAMES TATTOOS
OPERAS SAMOAN
BRAIN DATER WAG
BOCA COVEN GERE
SNO DOVER CRETE
    NEEDED THAMES
PAJAMAS GRASSLE
AMORE MIEN
NIN REVERENDJIM
INE IDEAL ERICA
COS TEXTS LUGER
```

6

```
LOLA TAIL MACS
ALOU ALSO BLAHS
VICTORIASSECRET
ANOINT YEW ONEA
    SCAT EATERY
MYSTERYGUEST
RONI ERUPTS YOB
EDUCE ASH TAUPE
DAB ISNTIT BRER
    KNOTSLANDING
MARIEL LUAU
ALID OAS TYCOBB
LEADINGQUESTION
LUTES RYAN OSSA
TADA IDES RENI
```

7

```
EMMA BABAR PACK
NEIL AHORA OGRE
DOLL REACT LEAN
WOOLGATHERING
COED ACTS
ATBAT SIEVE
SILT AVENGE MTS
PETERCOTTONTAIL
SRS AMIGOS ECRU
CREDO TAKER
SHOE LAIC
TERRYBRADSHAW
WARN ALICE ECHO
ALOE MODEL RUED
GENA SWEDE SPED
```

8

```
APSE CALEB AFAR
LIEN AROSE SLUE
BALDERDASH SANG
AFFORDED ADAPTS
    WREN OVOID
STEED GRIDLOCK
CHORD MAGOO ORE
HEMS CIGAR ODIN
OAF PREEN MULES
PROTEINS DATED
    OUSTS DAMP
POLLOI AIRBUSES
ONEL CODSWALLOP
ETRE ABACI LANA
TOYS LEMON SYST
```

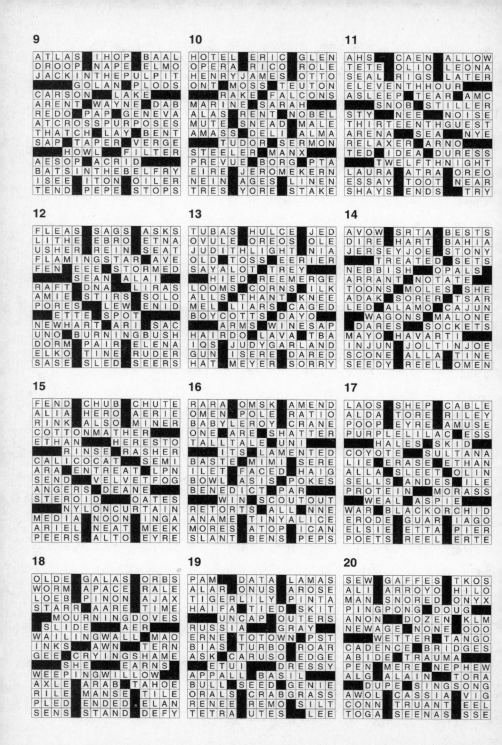

9

```
ATLAS  IHOP   BAAL
DROOP  NAPE   ELMO
JACKINTHEPULPIT
    GOLAN  PLODS
CARSON    LAKE
ARENT  WAYNE  DAB
REDO  PAP  GENEVA
ATCROSSPURPOSES
THATCH  LAY  BENT
SAP  TAPER  VERGE
   HOWL  FILTER
AESOP  ACRID
BATSINTHEBELFRY
ISEE  ITON  OILER
TEND  PEPE  STOPS
```

10

```
HOTEL  ERIC   GLEN
OPERA  RICO   ROLE
HENRYJAMES   OTTO
ONT   MOSS  TEUTON
    RAKE  FALCONS
MARINE   SARAH
ALAS  RENT  NOBEL
MUTE  SNEAD  MALE
AMASS  DELI  ALMA
   TUDOR  SERMON
STEELER   MANX
PREVUE  BORG  PTA
EIRE  JEROMEKERN
NEIN  AGES  LINEN
TRES  YORE  STAKE
```

11

```
AHS   CAEN   ALLOW
TETE  OLIO   LEONA
SEAL  RIGS   LATER
ELEVENTHHOUR
ASLEEP  TEAR  AMC
    SNOB  STILLER
STY  NEE  NOISE
THIRTEENTHGUEST
ARENA   SEA  NYE
RELAXER   ARNO
TED  IDEA  DURESS
   TWELFTHNIGHT
LAURA  ATRA  OREO
ESSAY  TOOT  NEAR
SHAYS  ENDS  TRY
```

12

```
FLEAS  SAGS   ASKS
LITHE  EBRO   ETNA
USHER  REIN   SEAT
FLAMINGSTAR  AVE
FEN  EEE  STORMED
   SEAN  ALAI
RAFT  DNA  LIRAS
AMIE  STIRS  SOLO
PORES  LEW  ENID
   ETTE  SPOT
NEWHART  ARI  SAC
UNO  BURNINGBUSH
DORM  PAIR  ELENA
ELKO  TINE  RUDER
SASE  SLED  SEERS
```

13

```
TUBAS  HULCE   JED
OVULE  OREOS   OLE
JUDITHLIGHT   NIA
OLD  TOSS  EERIER
SAYALOT   TREY
HIED  REEMERGE
LOOMS  CORNS  ILK
ALLS  THANT  KNEE
MEL  LIARS  CAGED
BOYCOTTS   DAYO
ARMS  WINESAP
HAIRDO  LAVA  TBA
IQS  JUDYGARLAND
GUN  ISERE  DARED
HAT  MEYER  SORRY
```

14

```
AVOW  SRTA   BESTS
DIRE  HART   BAHIA
JERSEYJOE   STONY
   TREATED   SETS
NEBBISH   OPALS
ARRANT   NOTATE
TOONS  MOLES  SHE
ADAK  SORER  TSAR
LED  ALAMO  CAJUN
   WAGONS  MALONE
DARES   SOCKETS
MAYO   HAVARTI
INJUN  JOLTINJOE
SCONE  ALLA  TINE
SEEDY  REEL  OMEN
```

15

```
FEND  CHUB   CHUTE
ALIA  HERO   AERIE
RINK  ALSO   MINER
COTTONMATHER
ETHAN   HERESTO
   RINSE  RASHER
CALICOCAT   SEMI
ARA  ENTREAT  LPN
SEND  VELVETFOG
ANGERS   DEANE
STEROID   OATES
NYLONCURTAIN
MEDIA  NOON  INGA
ARIEL  NEAT  MEEK
PEERS  ALTO  EYRE
```

16

```
RARA  OMSK   AMEND
OMEN  POLE   RATIO
BABYLEROY   CRANE
ONE  ARE  SHATTER
TALLTALE   UNI
   ITS  LAMENTED
BASTE  MIMI  SERE
ILET  FACED  HAIG
BOWL  ASIS  POKES
BENEDICT   PAR
   WIN  SCOUTOUT
RETORTS  ALL  NNE
ANAME  TINYALICE
MORES  ATOP  ICAN
SLANT  BENS  PEPS
```

17

```
LAOS  SHEP   CABLE
ALDA  TORE   RILEY
POOP  EYRE   AMUSE
PURPLELILAC   ESS
   HALES  SKID
COYOTE   SULTANA
LIE  ERASE  ETHAN
ALLA  SLEET  OLIN
SELLS  ANDES  ILE
PROTEIN   MORASS
WEAL   ASPIE
WAR  BLACKORCHID
ERODE  GUAR  IAGO
ELSIE  ETTA  PIER
POETS  REEL  ERTE
```

18

```
OLDE  GALAS   ORBS
WORM  APACE   RALE
LOEB  PINON   AJAX
STARR  AARE   TIME
MOURNINGDOVES
SLIDE   AER
WAILINGWALL  MAO
INKS  AWN  TERN
GEE  CRYINGSHAME
   SHE  EARNS
WEEPINGWILLOW
AXLE  ARAB  TAHOE
RILE  MANSE  TILE
PLED  ENDED  ELAN
SENS  STAND  DEFY
```

19

```
PAM   DATA   LAMAS
ALAR  ONUS   AROSE
TIGERLILY   PINTA
HAIFA  TIED  SKIT
   UNCAP  OUTERS
RUSSIA   GRAY
ERNE  TOTOWN  PST
BIAS  TURBO  ROAR
ASK  CARUSO  EDGE
   ETUI  DRESSY
APPALL   BASIL
BULL  SEED  GENIE
ORALS  CRABGRASS
RENEE  REMO  SILT
TETRA  UTES  LEE
```

20

```
SEW   GAFFES  TKOS
ALI   ARROYO  HILO
MAN   SNORED  ONYX
PINGPONG   DOUG
ANON  DOZEN  KLM
NEWAGE  NONE  OOO
   WETTER  TANGO
CADENCE   BRIDGES
ABIDE   TRAUMA
PEN  MERE  NEPHEW
ALG  ALAIN  TORA
DUPE  SINGSONG
AWOL  CASSIA  VIG
CONN  TRUANT  EEL
TOGA  SEENAS  SSE
```

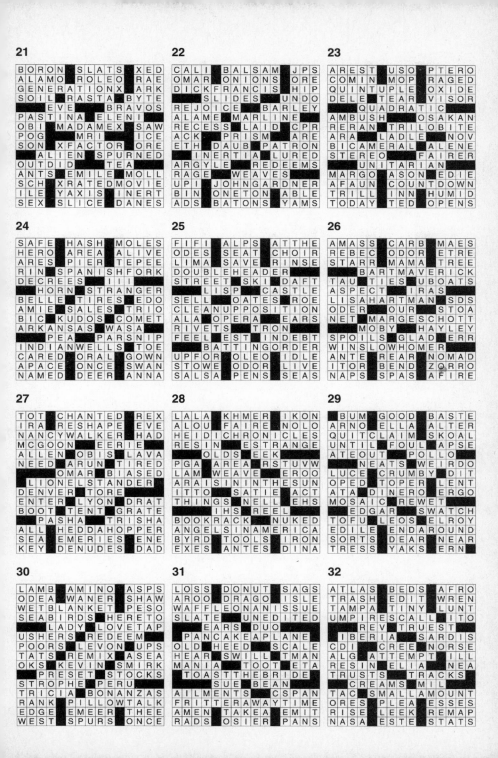

21

B	O	R	O	N		S	L	A	T	S		X	E	D
A	L	A	M	O		R	O	L	E	O		R	A	E
G	E	N	E	R	A	T	I	O	N	X		A	R	K
S	O	I	L		R	A	S	T	A		B	Y	T	E
			E	V	E				B	R	A	V	O	S
P	A	S	T	I	N	A		E	L	E	N	I		
O	B	I		M	A	D	A	M	E	X		S	A	W
P	O	G			M	R	I			I	C	E		
S	O	N		X	F	A	C	T	O	R		O	R	E
		A	L	I	E	N		S	P	U	R	N	E	D
O	U	T	D	I	D			T	E	A				
A	N	T	S		E	M	I	L	E		M	O	L	L
S	C	H		X	R	A	T	E	D	M	O	V	I	E
I	L	E		Y	A	X	I	S		I	N	E	R	T
S	E	X		S	L	I	C	E		D	A	N	E	S

22

C	A	L	I		B	A	L	S	A	M		J	P	S
O	M	A	R		O	N	I	O	N	S		O	R	E
D	I	C	K	F	R	A	N	C	I	S		H	I	P
			S	L	I	D	E	S			U	N	D	O
R	E	J	O	I	C	E			B	A	R	L	E	Y
A	L	A	M	E		M	A	R	L	I	N	E		
R	E	C	E	S	S		L	A	I	D		C	P	R
A	C	K		P	R	I	S	M			A	R	E	
E	T	H		D	A	U	B		P	A	T	R	O	N
			I	N	E	R	T	I	A		L	U	R	E	D
A	R	G	Y	L	E			R	E	D	E	E	M	S
R	A	G	E			W	E	A	V	E	S			
U	P	I		J	O	H	N	G	A	R	D	N	E	R
B	I	N		O	N	E	T	O	N		A	B	L	E
A	D	S		B	A	T	O	N	S		Y	A	M	S

23

A	R	E	S	T		U	S	O		P	T	E	R	O
C	O	M	I	N		M	O	P		R	A	G	E	D
Q	U	I	N	T	U	P	L	E		O	X	I	D	E
D	E	L	E		T	E	A	R		V	I	S	O	R
				Q	U	A	D	R	A	T	I	C		
A	M	B	U	S	H				O	S	A	K	A	N
R	E	R	A	N		T	R	I	L	O	B	I	T	E
A	R	A		L	A	D	L	E				N	O	V
B	I	C	A	M	E	R	A	L		A	L	E	N	E
S	T	E	R	E	O			F	A	I	R	E	R	
			U	N	I	T	A	R	I	A	N			
M	A	R	G	O		A	S	O	N		E	D	I	E
A	F	A	U	N		C	O	U	N	T	D	O	W	N
T	R	I	L	L		I	N	N		H	U	M	I	D
T	O	D	A	Y		T	E	D		O	P	E	N	S

24

S	A	F	E		H	A	S	H		M	O	L	E	S
H	E	R	O		A	R	E	A		A	L	I	V	E
A	R	E	S		P	I	E	R		T	E	P	E	E
R	I	N		S	P	A	N	I	S	H	F	O	R	K
D	E	C	R	E	E	S			I	I	I			
			H	O	R	N		S	T	R	A	N	G	E	R
B	E	L	L	E		T	I	R	E	S		E	D	O
A	M	I	E		S	A	L	E	S		T	R	I	O
B	I	C		K	U	D	O	S		C	O	M	E	T
A	R	K	A	N	S	A	S		W	A	S	A		
			P	E	A			P	A	R	S	N	I	P
I	N	D	I	A	N	W	E	L	L	S		T	O	E
C	A	R	E	D		O	R	A	L		G	O	W	N
A	P	A	C	E		O	N	C	E		S	W	A	N
N	A	M	E	D		D	E	E	R		A	N	N	A

25

F	I	F	I		A	L	P	S		A	T	T	H	E
O	D	E	S		S	E	A	T		C	H	O	I	R
L	I	M	A		S	A	V	E		R	I	N	S	E
D	O	U	B	L	E	H	E	A	D	E	R			
S	T	R	E	E	T		S	K	I		D	A	F	T
			L	I	S	P			C	A	S	T	L	E
S	E	L	L		O	A	T	E	S		R	O	E	
C	L	E	A	N	U	P	P	O	S	I	T	I	O	N
A	L	A		O	P	E	R	A		E	A	R	S	
R	I	V	E	T	S			T	R	O	N			
F	E	E	L		E	S	T		I	N	D	E	B	T
			B	A	T	T	I	N	G	O	R	D	E	R
U	P	F	O	R		O	L	E	O		I	D	L	E
S	T	O	W	E		O	D	O	R		L	I	V	E
S	A	L	S	A		P	E	N	S		S	E	A	S

26

A	M	A	S	S		C	A	R	B		M	A	E	S
R	E	B	E	C		O	D	O	R		E	T	R	E
S	T	A	R	R		M	A	M	A		T	R	E	E
			B	A	R	T	M	A	V	E	R	I	C	K
T	A	U		T	I	E	S			U	B	O	A	T	S
A	S	P	E	C	T				I	R	A	S		
L	I	S	A	H	A	R	T	M	A	N		S	D	S
O	D	E	R			O	U	R			S	T	O	A
N	E	T		M	A	R	G	E	S	C	H	O	T	T
			M	O	B	Y			H	A	Y	L	E	Y
S	P	O	I	L	S			G	L	A	D		E	R	R
W	I	N	S	L	O	W	H	O	M	E	R			
A	N	T	E		R	E	A	R		N	O	M	A	D
I	T	O	R		B	E	N	D		Z	O	R	R	O
N	A	P	S		S	P	A	S		A	F	I	R	E

27

T	O	T		C	H	A	N	T	E	D		R	E	X
I	R	A		R	E	S	H	A	P	E		E	V	E
N	A	N	C	Y	W	A	L	K	E	R		H	A	D
M	C	G	O	O	N			E	E	R	I	E		
A	L	L	E	N		O	B	I	S		L	A	V	A
N	E	E	D		A	R	U	N		T	I	R	E	D
			O	M	A	R		B	I	A	S	E	D	
L	I	O	N	E	L	S	T	A	N	D	E	R		
D	E	N	V	E	R			T	O	R	E			
E	N	T	E	R		L	Y	O	N		D	R	A	T
B	O	O	T		T	E	N	T		G	R	A	T	E
			P	A	S	H	A		T	R	I	S	H	A
A	L	L		H	E	D	D	A	H	O	P	P	E	R
S	E	A		E	M	E	R	I	E	S		E	N	E
K	E	Y		D	E	N	U	D	E	S		D	A	D

28

L	A	L	A		K	H	M	E	R		I	K	O	N
A	L	O	U		F	A	I	R	E		N	O	L	O
H	E	I	D	I	C	H	R	O	N	I	C	L	E	S
R	E	S	I	N			E	S	T	R	A	N	G	E
			O	L	D	S			E	E	K			
P	G	A		A	R	E	A		R	S	T	U	V	W
L	A	M		W	E	A	V	E		E	R	O	O	
A	R	A	I	S	I	N	I	N	T	H	E	S	U	N
I	T	T	O		S	A	T	I	E		A	C	T	
T	H	I	N	G	S		N	E	L	L		E	H	S
			I	H	S			R	E	E	L			
B	O	O	K	R	A	C	K		N	U	K	E	D	
A	N	G	E	L	S	I	N	A	M	E	R	I	C	A
B	Y	R	D		T	O	O	L	S		I	R	O	N
E	X	E	S		A	N	T	E	S		D	I	N	A

29

B	U	M		G	O	O	D		B	A	S	T	E
A	R	N	O		E	L	L	A		A	L	T	E	R
Q	U	I	T	C	L	A	I	M		S	K	O	A	L
U	N	T	I	L		F	O	U	L		A	P	S	E
A	T	E	O	U	T				P	O	L	L	O	
			N	E	A	T	S		W	E	I	R	D	O
L	U	C	E		C	R	U	M	B	Y		D	I	T
O	P	E	D		T	O	P	E	R		L	E	N	T
A	T	A		D	I	N	E	R	O		E	R	G	O
M	O	S	A	I	C			R	E	W	E	T		
			E	D	G	A	R			S	W	A	T	C	H
T	O	F	U		L	E	O	S		E	L	R	O	Y
E	D	I	L	E		E	N	D	A	R	O	U	N	D
S	O	R	T	S		D	E	A	R		N	E	A	R
T	R	E	S	S		Y	A	K	S		E	R	N	

30

L	A	M	B		A	M	I	N	O		A	S	P	S
O	D	E	A		W	A	N	E	R		S	H	A	W
W	E	T	B	L	A	N	K	E	T		P	E	S	O
S	E	A	B	I	R	D	S		H	E	R	E	T	O
			L	A	D	Y		L	O	V	E	T	A	P
U	S	H	E	R	S		R	E	D	E	E	M		
P	O	O	R	S		L	E	V	O	N		U	P	S
T	A	T	S		R	E	M	I	X		A	S	E	A
O	K	S		K	E	V	I	N		S	M	I	R	K
			P	R	E	S	E	T		S	T	O	C	K	S
S	T	R	O	P	H	E		P	E	R	U			
T	R	I	C	I	A		B	O	N	A	N	Z	A	S
R	A	N	K		P	I	L	L	O	W	T	A	L	K
E	D	G	E		E	M	E	E	R		T	H	E	E
W	E	S	T		S	P	U	R	S		O	N	C	E

31

L	O	S	S		D	O	N	U	T		S	A	G	S
A	R	O	O		D	R	A	G	O		I	S	L	E
W	A	F	F	L	E	O	N	A	N	I	S	S	U	E
S	L	A	T	E			U	N	E	D	I	T	E	D
			E	A	R	S			D	U	O			
P	A	N	C	A	K	E	A	P	L	A	N	E		
O	L	D		H	E	E	D		S	C	A	L	E	
H	E	A	R		S	W	I	L	L		T	M	A	N
M	A	N	I	A			T	O	O	T		E	T	A
			T	O	A	S	T	T	H	E	B	R	I	D	E
S	U	E		B	E	A	N							
A	I	L	M	E	N	T	S			C	S	P	A	N
F	R	I	T	T	E	R	A	W	A	Y	T	I	M	E
A	M	E	N		T	A	K	E	A		E	M	I	T
R	A	D	S		O	S	I	E	R		P	A	N	S

32

A	T	L	A	S		B	E	D	S		A	F	R	O
T	R	A	S	H		E	D	I	T		W	R	E	N
T	A	M	P	A		T	I	N	Y		L	U	N	T
U	M	P	I	R	E	S	C	A	L	L		I	T	O
			R	E	V			T	R	U	E	S	T		
I	B	E	R	I	A				S	A	R	D	I	S
C	D	I		C	R	E	E			N	O	R	S	E
A	L	G		A	T	T	E	M	P	T		I	L	L
R	E	S	I	N		E	L	I	A		N	E	A	
			T	R	U	S	T	S		T	R	A	C	K	S
			C	R	E	A	M	S		M	I	L		
T	A	C		S	M	A	L	L	A	M	O	U	N	T
O	R	E	S		P	L	E	A		E	S	S	E	S
R	I	S	E		L	E	E	K		R	E	M	A	P
N	A	S	A		E	S	T	E		S	T	A	T	S

33

H	A	F	T	S	■	S	H	E	M	■	A	G	A	R
A	P	I	A	N	■	T	E	M	A	■	N	E	R	O
D	I	S	C	O	■	R	E	I	N	■	T	O	D	O
J	A	C	K	O	F	A	L	L	T	R	A	D	E	S
■	■	■	Z	A	P	■	■	R	E	G	E	N	T	■
C	A	S	P	E	R	■	A	B	A	C	O	■	■	■
O	D	E	R	■	G	I	L	A	■	O	N	T	O	P
Q	U	E	E	N	O	F	T	H	E	N	I	G	H	T
S	E	N	S	E	■	F	O	N	T	■	S	I	N	E
■	■	■	S	T	A	Y	S	■	H	O	T	F	O	R
■	S	H	O	A	T	S	■	■	R	I	M	■	■	■
K	I	N	G	O	F	T	H	E	C	A	S	T	L	E
U	N	I	E	■	A	R	A	B	■	H	E	R	O	N
A	G	O	N	■	T	A	R	E	■	A	M	E	N	D
S	E	N	T	■	E	P	I	C	■	N	I	K	E	S

34

T	R	A	D	E	R	■	S	P	A	M	■	C	A	M
B	E	M	I	N	E	■	L	A	N	E	■	A	M	A
S	M	O	K	E	S	■	E	R	A	S	■	W	O	N
P	O	K	E	R	C	H	E	E	P	S	■	W	E	D
■	■	■	■	G	O	A	T	E	E	■	B	A	B	E
O	O	H	■	Y	R	S	■	■	S	E	R	I	A	L
C	H	O	O	■	E	N	D	■	T	O	O	T	■	■
T	O	O	D	Y	■	T	O	P	■	S	N	I	D	E
■	■	T	O	A	D	■	T	R	I	■	K	N	E	W
M	A	T	U	R	E	■	■	I	N	K	■	G	E	E
O	R	A	L	■	■	B	R	A	C	C	O	■	■	■
N	A	M	■	Q	U	A	C	K	E	R	J	A	C	K
I	R	A	■	U	S	N	A	■	N	E	E	S	O	N
C	A	L	■	I	S	I	S	■	S	A	L	I	N	E
A	T	E	■	T	Y	N	E	■	E	N	L	A	C	E

35

S	I	S	■	V	E	N	A	L	■	C	H	I	T	■
A	N	E	W	■	A	M	A	N	A	■	O	E	N	O
V	O	C	A	L	C	O	R	D	S	■	R	A	G	E
E	N	T	R	E	A	T	Y	■	T	R	A	D	E	D
■	■	■	D	E	S	P	I	T	E	■	S	W	E	L	L
■	A	G	E	■	S	H	O	P	■	I	M	P	■	■
N	I	N	T	H	■	P	I	E	R	S	■	N	I	A
U	H	O	H	■	S	A	T	E	D	■	C	E	N	T
D	A	S	■	R	A	N	U	P	■	S	U	S	I	E
■	■	E	D	T	■	O	W	E	S	■	T	O	R	■
■	■	R	O	O	T	S	■	C	A	B	A	R	E	T
S	T	I	N	K	O	■	S	O	M	E	T	I	M	E
P	A	N	T	■	O	N	T	H	E	R	O	P	E	S
A	R	G	O	■	T	R	E	E	S	■	R	E	N	T
R	A	S	P	■	H	A	S	N	T	■	R	D	S	■

36

D	E	S	I	■	S	P	L	A	T	■	A	T	I	T
E	R	A	T	■	P	A	U	L	A	■	M	A	R	E
L	I	F	E	J	A	C	K	E	T	■	P	T	A	S
I	C	E	M	A	N	■	E	X	E	C	U	T	E	S
■	■	■	I	N	K	S	■	■	R	O	L	L	■	■
A	D	Z	E	■	E	L	M	■	H	E	E	D	S	■
W	I	R	E	■	F	R	E	E	Z	E	■	T	O	E
O	N	E	S	W	R	I	T	T	E	N	N	A	M	E
U	T	A	■	R	O	A	M	E	D	■	A	L	E	S
■	K	I	R	B	Y	■	L	E	O	■	T	U	E	S
■	■	I	R	E	S	■	■	R	O	O	T	■	■	■
G	E	N	E	R	O	U	S	■	U	N	I	O	N	S
I	D	E	A	■	F	R	E	E	T	I	C	K	E	T
F	I	S	T	■	A	G	A	T	E	■	A	R	E	A
T	E	S	H	■	S	E	N	O	R	■	L	A	D	Y

37

S	M	E	W	■	A	B	R	A	M	■	D	I	E	T
H	O	B	O	■	D	O	O	N	E	■	O	N	C	E
E	V	E	L	■	O	S	S	I	E	■	E	T	R	E
A	I	R	F	O	R	C	E	O	N	E	■	H	U	M
■	■	■	R	E	T	I	N	A	■	N	I	C	H	E
■	■	S	O	B	E	R	■	■	E	L	A	N	D	S
M	A	T	H	■	L	A	I	R	■	A	M	A	R	A
A	C	H	■	S	E	R	V	A	N	T	■	V	A	N
R	A	I	T	T	■	N	E	M	O	■	B	Y	T	E
S	T	R	E	E	P	■	■	T	A	B	L	E	■	■
■	■	■	D	E	A	L	T	■	L	I	E	G	E	S
S	P	A	■	M	A	R	I	N	E	S	H	Y	M	N
C	U	R	L	■	S	O	D	O	M	■	I	R	M	A
A	M	M	O	■	M	O	O	R	E	■	V	E	E	R
M	A	Y	S	■	A	P	L	A	N	■	E	S	T	E

38

D	I	S	C	■	L	I	M	A	N	■	A	C	O	P
U	L	N	A	■	E	D	I	N	A	■	R	U	L	E
G	O	E	R	■	N	O	S	E	T	A	C	K	L	E
U	V	E	A	L	■	E	M	I	T	■	E	A	R	■
P	E	R	F	U	M	E	R	I	V	E	R	■	■	■
■	■	■	E	L	I	S	■	C	E	N	A	C	L	E
F	O	B	■	L	E	A	N	■	■	N	O	I	R	■
D	R	U	G	S	N	I	F	F	I	N	G	D	O	G
■	I	S	L	A	■	■	L	E	N	O	■	A	N	O
C	O	L	L	E	G	E	■	A	C	T	E	■	■	■
■	■	■	A	R	O	M	A	T	H	E	R	A	P	Y
A	W	E	■	A	S	P	S	■	■	D	O	B	R	O
L	O	V	E	S	T	I	N	K	S	■	T	O	O	K
G	R	E	G	■	A	R	E	E	L	■	I	D	L	E
A	E	R	O	■	G	E	R	R	Y	■	C	E	E	S

39

W	A	L	E	S	■	B	O	T	H	■	S	A	S	K
A	P	A	R	T	■	A	L	E	E	■	E	G	A	N
L	I	B	R	A	■	N	E	A	L	■	S	O	B	E
L	E	O	■	M	A	J	O	R	L	E	A	G	U	E
■	■	R	O	M	E	O	■	■	G	E	M	■	■	■
L	O	U	V	E	R	■	S	T	A	G	E	S	E	T
A	S	N	E	R	■	E	T	A	T	S	■	I	R	E
S	T	I	R	■	A	D	E	L	E	■	C	E	N	T
T	E	O	■	A	N	G	E	L	■	M	A	R	I	O
S	O	N	G	S	T	E	R	■	B	A	R	R	E	N
■	■	■	L	I	E	■	■	M	A	N	T	A	■	■
C	A	P	I	T	A	L	G	A	N	G	■	C	P	O
F	R	E	D	■	T	E	A	L	■	E	L	L	E	N
O	G	R	E	■	E	V	I	L	■	R	O	U	T	E
S	O	U	R	■	R	I	L	E	■	S	O	B	E	R

40

R	A	N	T	■	E	W	E	L	L	■	T	S	A	R
A	L	O	U	■	M	A	R	I	A	■	R	E	N	O
F	L	A	X	■	P	R	I	N	T	■	A	L	T	O
■	S	H	E	R	L	O	C	K	H	O	L	M	E	S
■	■	■	D	I	O	N	■	■	Y	E	A	S	T	■
C	A	N	O	P	Y	■	■	C	A	B	L	E	■	■
A	D	I	E	U	■	S	H	I	M	■	■	O	D	S
L	O	R	D	P	E	T	E	R	W	I	M	S	E	Y
C	A	L	■	■	I	S	O	■	G	I	V	E	■	M	A	H	A	L
M	I	A	M	I	■	■	I	V	O	R	Y	■	B	A	C	A	L	L
I	N	S	P	E	C	T	O	R	M	O	R	S	E	■
N	A	P	A	■	H	O	R	E	B	■	O	O	Z	E
O	N	E	R	■	A	R	E	N	A	■	N	O	I	R
R	E	N	T	■	D	O	O	D	Y	■	I	N	O	N

41

L	I	M	B	■	I	M	E	T	A	■	B	O	S	H
O	N	E	A	■	D	R	A	W	L	■	A	L	T	O
T	U	R	K	E	Y	T	R	O	T	■	L	E	A	N
U	R	I	E	L	■	■	S	W	A	N	S	O	N	G
S	E	T	S	O	F	F	■	A	R	I	A	■	■	■
■	■	■	R	O	R	Y	■	■	A	M	I	S	H	■
E	S	S	■	B	O	L	O	■	I	C	I	C	L	E
T	H	E	F	U	N	K	Y	C	H	I	C	K	E	N
T	O	L	A	S	T	■	A	L	A	N	■	Y	D	S
■	A	D	L	I	B	■	■	S	L	A	V	■	■	■
■	■	■	R	O	O	T	■	M	E	E	T	S	U	P
B	U	N	N	Y	H	O	P	■	M	A	I	N	E	■
E	R	I	E	■	G	O	O	S	E	S	T	E	P	S
T	A	N	S	■	O	G	L	E	R	■	U	N	I	T
A	L	E	S	■	D	E	L	T	A	■	M	A	N	O

42

F	U	M	E	■	K	A	R	M	A	■	A	B	U	T
E	T	O	N	■	U	S	U	A	L	■	K	A	N	E
W	A	L	T	■	R	O	S	S	I	■	I	L	I	E
■	H	E	R	M	A	N	S	H	E	R	M	I	T	S
■	■	■	A	I	L	■	■	N	U	B	■	■	■	■
I	W	A	N	T	T	O	B	E	A	L	O	N	E	■
F	O	R	C	E	■	C	A	T	T	Y	■	E	X	T
F	O	I	E	■	M	O	S	H	E	■	M	A	C	E
Y	E	S	■	C	U	M	I	N	■	O	A	T	E	N
■	R	E	M	O	T	E	C	O	N	T	R	O	L	S
■	■	■	A	D	A	■	■	O	H	M	■	■	■	■
I	S	O	L	A	T	I	O	N	B	O	O	T	H	■
N	O	V	A	■	I	N	D	I	E	■	S	H	A	Q
C	H	A	D	■	O	F	A	L	L	■	E	A	V	E
H	O	L	Y	■	N	O	Y	E	S	■	T	I	E	D

43

D	I	N	E	S	■	A	T	T	A	■	S	E	R	A
A	D	E	L	E	■	L	O	O	N	■	E	N	I	D
N	E	W	B	E	D	F	O	R	D	■	O	D	D	S
E	S	■	C	A	T	E	R	E	R	■	I	S	S	U	E
S	■	E	T	O	■	S	E	E	P	■	C	L	A	M	S
D	E	N	G	■	D	A	T	E	R	■	V	A	T	■
■	E	E	L	■	D	I	L	A	T	O	R	Y	■	■
K	E	N	N	E	B	U	N	K	P	O	R	T	■	■
G	A	L	A	C	T	I	C	■	S	E	T	■	■	■
I	L	E	■	O	S	C	A	R	■	S	C	A	M	■
N	E	V	E	R	■	H	I	L	O	■	A	N	A
■	A	D	E	P	T	■	S	E	M	I	N	A	R	■
A	N	T	I	■	H	A	C	K	E	N	S	A	C	K
L	O	O	T	■	I	L	I	E	■	I	N	D	I	E
E	R	R	S	■	L	E	A	D	■	S	T	A	N	D

44

B	A	S	E	■	C	H	E	T	■	P	O	S	S	E
A	R	I	D	■	H	U	G	O	■	A	R	E	N	A
N	C	A	A	■	A	S	A	P	■	L	I	N	U	S
C	O	M	M	O	N	K	N	O	W	L	E	D	G	E
■	■	■	B	E	Y	■	■	H	E	N	■	■	■	■
C	A	G	N	E	Y	■	A	B	E	T	T	O	R	S
O	G	E	E	S	■	L	I	L	■	■	P	O	O	■
M	A	T	T	E	R	O	F	O	P	I	N	I	O	N
B	I	T	■	■	A	N	I	■	D	O	N	N	A	■
S	N	O	W	S	H	O	E	■	C	A	R	E	E	R
■	■	■	O	N	A	■	■	O	O	H	■	■	■	■
S	C	H	O	O	L	O	F	T	H	O	U	G	H	T
P	A	O	L	O	■	A	L	T	O	■	G	L	E	E
I	S	L	E	T	■	T	E	E	S	■	L	A	R	A
T	E	E	N	Y	■	H	A	R	T	■	I	D	E	S

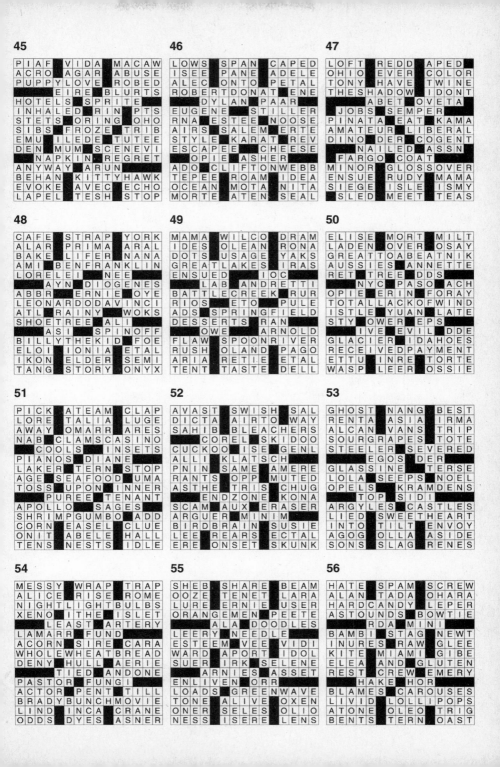

45

```
PIAF . VIDA . MACAW
ACRO . AGAR . ABUSE
PUPPYLOVE . ROBED
... EIRE . BLURTS
HOTELS . SPRITE .
INHALED . RIN . PTS
STETS . ORING . OHO
SIBS . FROZE . TRIB
EMU . ILEDE . TUTEE
DEN . MUM . SCENEVI
. NAPKIN . REGRET
ANYWAY . ARUN ...
BEHAN . KITTYHAWK
EVOKE . AVEC . ECHO
LAPEL . TESH . STOP
```

46

```
LOWS . SPAN . CAPED
ISEE . PANE . ADELE
ALEC . ONTO . PETAL
ROBERTDONAT . ENE
DYLAN . PAAR ...
EUGENE . STILLER
RNA . ESTEE . NOOSE
AIRS . SALEM . ERTE
STYLE . KARAT . REV
ESCAPEE . CHEESE
... OPIE . ASHER
ADO . CLIFTONWEBB
TEPEE . ROAM . IDEA
OCEAN . MOTA . NITA
MORTE . ATEN . SEAL
```

47

```
LOFT . REDD . APED
OHIO . EVER . COLOR
TONY . HAVE . TWINE
THESHADOW . IDONT
... ABET . OVETA
JOBS . SEMPER ...
PINATA . EAT . KAMA
AMATEUR . LIBERAL
DINO . DER . COGENT
. NAILED . ASSN
... FARGO . COAT
MINOR . GLOSSOVER
ENSUE . RUDY . MAMA
SIEGE . ISLE . ISMY
. SLED . MEET . TEAS
```

48

```
CAFE . STRAP . YORK
ALAR . PRIMA . ARAL
BAKE . LIFER . NANA
AMI . BENFRANKLIN
LORELEI . NEE ...
. AYN . DIOGENES
ABBR . ERNIE . OYE
LEONARDODAVINCI
ATL . RAINY . WOKS
SHOETREE . ALI .
... ASI . SPINOFF
BILLYTHEKID . FOE
ELOI . IONIA . ETAL
IKON . ELDER . SEMI
TANG . STORY . ONYX
```

49

```
MAMA . WILCO . DRAM
IDES . OLEAN . RONA
DOTS . USAGE . YAKS
GREATLAKES . IRAS
ENSUED . IOC ...
... LAB . ANDRETTI
BATTLECREEK . RUR
RIOS . ETO . PULE
ADS . SPRINGFIELD
DESSERTS . RAN ...
. OWE . ARNOLD
FLAW . SPOONRIVER
RUSH . OLAND . PAGO
ARIA . RETIE . ETAL
TENT . TASTE . DELL
```

50

```
ELISE . MORT . MILT
LADEN . OVER . OSAY
GREATTOABEATNIK
AUSSIES . ANNETTE
RET . TREE . DDS ...
... NYC . PASO . ACH
OPIE . ERIN . FORAY
TOTALLACKOFWIND
ISTLE . YUAN . LATE
STY . OWER . EPS ...
... IVE . EVIL . DDE
GLACIER . IDAHOES
RECEIVEDPAYMENT
ETTU . INRE . TORTE
WASP . LEER . OSSIE
```

51

```
PICK . ATEAM . CLAP
LORE . TALIA . LUGE
AWAY . OMARR . ARES
NAB . CLAMSCASINO
. COOLS . INSETS
PIANOS . DIANE ...
LAKER . TERN . STOP
AGE . SEAFOOD . UMA
TOSS . UPON . INNER
. PUREE . TENANT
APOLLO . SAGES ...
SHRIMPGUMBO . ADD
CORN . EASEL . CLUE
ONIT . ABELE . HALL
TENS . NESTS . IDLE
```

52

```
AVAST . SWISH . SAL
DICTA . AIRTO . WAY
SAHIB . BLEACHERS
... COREL . SKIDOO
CUCKOO . ISE . GENL
ALLI . KLATSCH ...
PNIN . SAME . AMERE
RANTS . OPP . MUTED
ASTHE . TRIS . CHUG
... ENDZONE . KONA
SCAM . AUX . ERASER
ARGUER . MINIM ...
BIRDBRAIN . SUSIE
LEE . REARS . ECTAL
ERE . ONSET . SKUNK
```

53

```
GHOST . NANG . BEST
RENTA . ASIA . IRMA
ALCAN . VANS . TRIP
SOURGRAPES . TOTE
STEELER . SEVERED
... EGOS . DER ...
GLASSINE . TERSE
LOLA . SEEPS . NOEL
OPELS . KRAMDENS
. TOP . SIDI ...
ARGYLES . CASTLES
LIED . SWEETHEART
INTO . TILT . ENVOY
AGOG . OLLA . ASIDE
SONS . SLAG . RENES
```

54

```
MESSY . WRAP . TRAP
ALICE . RISE . ROME
NIGHTLIGHTBULBS
XENO . ITHE . ISLET
. LEAST . ARTERY
LAMARR . FUND ...
ACORN . SIRE . CARA
WHOLEWHEATBREAD
DENY . HULL . AERIE
... TIED . ANDONE
PASTOR . FUNGI ...
ACTOR . PENT . TILL
BRADYBUNCHMOVIE
LIND . INCA . CRANE
ODDS . DYES . ASNER
```

55

```
SHEB . SHARE . BEAM
OOZE . TENET . LARA
LURE . ERNIE . USER
ORANGEMEN . PEETE
... ALA . DOODLES
LEERY . NEEDLE ...
ESTEEM . VEE . VIDI
WARD . APORT . IDOL
SUER . IRK . SELENE
... ARNIES . ASSET
ENLIVEN . ORR ...
LOADS . GREENWAVE
TONE . ALIVE . OXEN
ONER . SELES . OLIO
NESS . ISERE . LENS
```

56

```
HATE . SPAM . SCREW
ALAN . TADA . OHARA
HARDCANDY . LEPER
ASTOUNDS . BOWTIE
... RDA . MINI ...
BAMBI . STAG . NEWT
INURES . RAW . GLEE
KITE . MIAMI . GIBE
ELEA . AND . GLUTEN
REST . CREW . EMERY
... HAKE . HOR ...
BLAMES . CAROUSES
LIVID . LOLLIPOPS
ATONE . OLEO . TRIG
BENTS . TERN . OAST
```

57

```
LEVI DADA  PASTA
ATOM ALOT  ROWAN
WHIPSMART  ERATO
NYC  ISNO BATTEN
SLEAZE  THECAT
   GIL HUSH ESS
HELEN EYRE  CAPO
ORANGES OTTOMAN
PAST ITIN  HASTY
ISH  EDEN CRT
LOVERS  RUSTIC
ERASER USES  AMO
RERAN SLAPHAPPY
GAUGE PALE  PEEL
SPEED ARTS  ORLY
```

58

```
RAG  DAB   ALDA
ERA OLIVES LEON
FIELDTRIPS AMIN
SALAD DREGS ONE
   BEG GETTING
SAP REMI   UND
HAILSTONE STROP
ERTE ZAIRE ROLE
SECTS SANDPAPER
HIP  REAL  SOT
RETIREE   MEA
WES NISEI ASSES
HEWN FALLSSHORT
AVON TUSSLE RIA
MEOW  ADD  TEN
```

59

```
LOTS NAPA  ROMA
ACHE OMENS EVIL
ITOR SANKA LENT
DOUBLESTANDARD
PJS  TEX
ARIOSO SEER PTA
BOLL BANNERYEAR
ALLES LEG YARNS
FLAGWAVERS LOGO
TOT ALAR HILTON
SIP  TRA
PENNANTWINNERS
ALMA CURIE AXEL
COIF ALECK GINA
ETTU LEES  STOW
```

60

```
LIDS  SLAVE AMPS
ANDI  CUMIN TALE
STABLECONDITION
SOY UNIS   NEST
GLEE  BESS
ATALL  MARITIME
SARA CARES  DOS
SHEDINHIBITIONS
EON NEONS  KLEE
SEAMLESS  RESTS
AIDE  TEAS
PENN MAXI  LEO
LODGEACOMPLAINT
OPIE SHAPE LEVI
BEER PETAL GUYS
```

61

```
LAPS ARCS   MOS
AGRAS DEAR PUNT
GOOSEBUMPS AREA
UNC NOSIR ARMOR
NIT SITTINGDUCK
AZORES  AGORAE
SERA SHARI  STY
HENPECKED
ARS ROARS  ABBA
RETAIN  FABLES
CHICKENFEED ALS
HILTS OILED CIA
ERLE COLDTURKEY
REED ISEE PEEVE
SSR  TERR  FRED
```

62

```
VERO DDTS  ELLE
ELAN CLOUT VOID
NEST OVULE ERMA
IMPOSSIBLEDREAM
PAT  LENNY
PHLOX AES ANENT
REEF AGO ISOMER
AMAT TERRE WIVE
MASHIE NOR ALEA
SNEER AOK INERT
WAIST  ADD
SECONDTHEMOTION
LAIR LAITY HOME
ORAL ERNES ETNA
PLOD DEGS  NAIL
```

63

```
IMAM LAPUP DADA
RAGA AMINO ELON
MARIAMONTESSORI
AMATI TOTE  HIT
ASTA  ITHACA
MARILYNMCCOO
EXO ENOCH NOBEL
TEXT ERRED DALI
ASYET AARON RAT
MICKEYMANTLE
CARPAL  LEOI
AGE RIAS  MCGEE
MICHAELMORIARTY
ELOI NAURU EIRE
LEND TIGER APED
```

64

```
RAPT AETNA VADE
ODER TRIES ARIL
PARISTEXAS LIAM
ELEVEN  IDEALS
RESIN  POISON
ATLANTICCITY
RPM OOZES  INRE
ALIGNS  ARAGON
MENU TESLA ETS
SANFRANCISCO
FACTOR  HUMID
RAMADA  RETUNE
AVOW CASABLANCA
GIVE IRANI GIAN
USED ATLAS ESNE
```

65

```
RASH STRAP TRAM
OTTO PRIMA AERO
STAB LASER KATE
AUTONICKNAME
ITT  LIONEL
PANGS  BALINESE
SARAH FUSE  ASA
TWENTIETHLETTER
ANN  SATE TEENS
REACTORS  SHANE
RESEAL  ALI
DRAINSECTION
TUBA TRITE IDLE
USER EATAT NEDS
GAGS SEARS TASS
```

66

```
HARP RIFT  METED
AMER INRE  ALIVE
LONI AFOX  SANER
FROMSTEMTOSTERN
ENACT  LEE
HASTA TOADS SUM
ATHIRD PPS MITE
FROMLEFTTORIGHT
TIRE SOO DINNER
SAT BIBBS DEERE
SAC  OUTOF
FROMLASTTOFIRST
LIVID ATUB EATA
AGATE GORY LYON
BALER AMES  DEWS
```

67

```
CLASP GOLF  SABE
ROPES EASE  TREX
EMPTYWORDS AIRE
PALACE  STRAND
ENE HBO   SEW
GOBBLEDEGOOK
JOUR EUR  EERIE
ESSES SEM DENSE
FLEET IGO  SEEN
FORKEDTONGUE
NAY  SAT   PAP
BONBON  OTELLO
AMOR DOUBLETALK
BANE ERNE RANEE
AROW RAID  STENS
```

68

```
TACOS SPOCK VCR
ABASH BERLE ALA
PERSONALDAY LON
STROVE TIM SLUG
BERT  EBBTIDE
SHOULDER  ALY
TALC RICKI  MOW
ALLOVERTHEPLACE
BEA AMAZE INTL
ZIP  YEARBOOK
SEMINAR  KLEE
PRIG THO GARAGE
RUM THINGAMAJIG
UPI DINTY ECOLE
ETC SCOOP REBAR
```

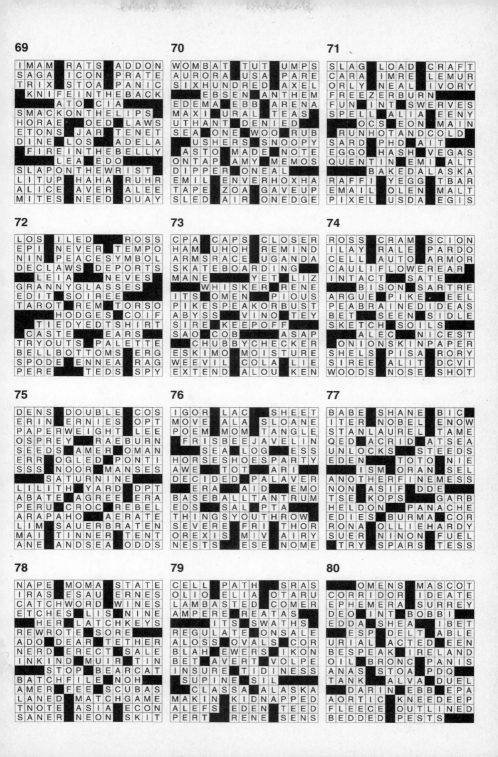

69

IMAM · RATS · ADDON
SAGA · ICON · PRATE
TRIX · STOA · PANIC
KNIFEINTHEBACK
· · ATO · CIA · ·
SMACKONTHELIPS
HORAE · OED · LAWS
ETONS · JAR · TENET
DINE · LOS · ADELA
FIREINTHEBELLY
· · LEA · EDO · ·
SLAPONTHEWRIST
LITUP · HAHA · RUHR
ALICE · AVER · ALEE
MITES · NEED · QUAY

70

WOMBAT · TUT · UMPS
AURORA · USA · PARE
SIXHUNDRED · AXEL
· · EBSEN · ANTHEM
EDEMA · EBB · ARENA
MAXI · URAL · TEAS
UTHANT · DENIED · ·
SEA · ONE · WOO · RUB
· · USHERS · SNOOPY
ASTO · MADE · NOTE
ONTAP · AMY · MEMOS
DIPPER · ONEAL · ·
EMIL · ENVERHOXHA
TAPE · ZOA · GAVEUP
SLED · AIR · ONEDGE

71

SLAG · LOAD · CRAFT
CARA · IMRE · LEMUR
ORLY · NEAL · IVORY
FREEZERBURN · · ·
FUN · INT · SWERVES
SPELL · ALIA · EENY
· · OCS · EON · MAIN
RUNHOTANDCOLD
SARD · PHD · AIT · ·
EGGO · HASH · VEGAS
QUENTIN · EMI · ALT
· · · BAKEDALASKA
RAFFI · YEGG · TBAR
EMAIL · OLEN · MALT
PIXEL · USDA · EGIS

72

LOS · ILED · · ROSS
EPI · NEVER · TEMPO
NIN · PEACESYMBOL
DECLAWS · DEPORTS
· · LEIA · NEVES · ·
GRANNYGLASSES
EDIT · SOIREE · · ·
TAROT · REM · TORSO
· · · HODGES · COIF
TIEDYEDTSHIRT
CASTE · · EARS · ·
TRYOUTS · PALETTE
BELLBOTTOMS · ERG
SPODE · ENNEA · RAG
PERE · · TEDS · SPY

73

CPA · CAPS · CLOSER
HAM · UHOH · REMIND
ARMSRACE · UGANDA
SKATEBOARDING
MANE · · YET · · LIZ
· WHISKER · RENE
ITS · OMEN · PIOUS
PIKESPEAKORBUST
ABYSS · VINO · TEY
SIRE · KEEPOFF · ·
SAO · COB · · ASAP
· CHUBBYCHECKER
ESKIMO · MOISTURE
WEEVIL · COLA · LIE
EXTEND · ALOU · KEN

74

ROSS · CRAM · SCION
ILAY · RALE · PARDO
CELL · AUTO · ARMOR
CAULIFLOWEREAR
INTACT · · SATE · ·
· · BISON · SARTRE
ARGUE · PIKE · EEL
PEABRAINEDIDEAS
BET · SEEN · SIDLE
SKETCH · SOILS · ·
· · ALEC · NICEST
ONIONSKINPAPER
SHELS · PISA · RORY
SIREE · ALIT · DCVI
WOODS · NOSE · SHOT

75

DENS · DOUBLE · COS
ERIN · ERNIES · OPT
PAPERWEIGHT · LEE
OSPREY · RAEBURN
SEEDS · AMER · OMAN
ERR · OGLED · PONTI
SSS · NOOR · MANSES
· · SATURNINE · ·
LILITH · YARD · DPT
ABATE · AGREE · ERA
PERU · CROC · REBEL
ARAPAHO · AERATE
LIM · SAUERBRATEN
MAI · TINNER · TENT
ANE · ANDSEA · ODDS

76

IGOR · LAC · SHEET
MOVE · ALA · SLOANE
POEM · MOM · TANGLE
FRISBEEJAVELIN
SEA · LOG · ESS · ·
HORSESHOESPARTY
AWE · TOT · ARI · ·
DECIDED · PALAVER
· · ERA · AID · EMO
BASEBALLTANTRUM
EDS · SAL · PTA · ·
THINGSYOUTHROW
SEVERE · FRI · THOR
OREXIS · MIV · AIRY
NESTS · ESE · NOME

77

BABE · SHANE · BIC
ITER · NOBEL · ENOW
STANLAUREL · TAME
QED · ACRID · ATSEA
UNLOCKS · STEEDS
EDEN · · TOTO · NIE
· · ISM · ORAN · SEL
ANOTHERFINEMESS
NON · ASIF · DDE · ·
TSE · KOPS · GARB
HELDON · PANACHE
EDIES · BURMA · COR
RONA · OLLIEHARDY
SUER · NINON · FUEL
TRY · SPARS · TESS

78

NAPE · MOMA · STATE
IRAS · ESAU · ERNES
CATCHWORD · WINES
ETCHES · LIS · NINE
· · HER · LATCHKEYS
REWROTE · SORE · ·
ADO · DEAR · TETHER
NERD · ERECT · SALE
INKIND · MUIR · TIN
· · STOP · BEARCAT
BATCHFILE · NOH
AMER · FEE · SCUBAS
LANED · MATCHGAME
TNOTE · ASIA · ECON
SANER · NEON · SKIT

79

CELL · PATH · SRAS
OLIO · ELIA · OTARU
LAMBASTED · COMER
AMPERE · REATAS
· · ITS · SWATHS
REGULATE · ONSALE
ALOSS · OVALS · COR
BLAH · EWERS · IKON
BET · AVERT · VOLPE
INSURE · TIDINESS
SUPINE · SIL · ·
CLASSA · ALASKA
MAKIN · KIDNAPPED
ALEFS · EDEN · TEED
PERT · RENE · SENS

80

· OMENS · MASCOT
CORRIDOR · IDEATE
EPHEMERA · SURREY
DEO · INT · BOBBI
EDDA · SHEA · IBET
· ESP · DELT · ABLE
URIAL · ACTED · EEN
BESPEAK · IRELAND
OIL · BRONC · PANIS
ANAS · STOA · PDQ
TANK · ALVA · DUEL
DARIN · EBB · EPA
AORTIC · KNEEDEEP
FLEECE · OUTLINED
BEDDED · PESTS

81

```
A D A N A   A L I     H A M
W I L T S   L O N     A L A
O N T H E T O W N   T B A R
I K E   A C H E   T H A N K
S E R B S   H A S B E E N
A N O R A K     E X P E R T
    I R A N I A N   I R O N
S I N G I N I N T H E R A I N
S T O A   S P A T U L A
S T A D I A     R A T T A N
H O T S E A T   M E A D E
P E S O S   P L E A   R E D
I V A N   C O V E R G I R L
C A R   I D I   M E L E E
A S K   T E N     S E E D S
```

82

```
A B A S H   S L A G   B L O B
C E L L O   T I L E   L U L U
D E M O N   A M I N   U S E R
C R A T E R L A K E   E T O N
      S E E   E V I L
S H O W T I M E   A R A F A T
I O N A   N A P S   A G A T E
E M I L   S T O P S   O L A N
G E O D E   E D I E   O S L O
E R N E S T   E N G I N E E R
      N A I L   N A M
S T E P   T I D A L B A S I N
O H I O   A M O K   I M A D E
F E R N   N I N E   B E L L A
T E E D   S T A R   E N T E R
```

83

```
S A M B A   M A P L E   O R R
T W I R L   O N I O N   C E O
A L L A B O U T E V E   E G O
      S E A S I D E   F L I T
M E L   E T S   S A L O M E
E X I T   M E A T   L A T E R
S P A R S E   R A B I N
S O M E C A M E R U N N I N G
      A R L E N   F E E D E R
A M A T I   W A I F   L O L A
D O R E M I   M A D   L L D
L I N D   N A T A L I E
I R E   A F E W G O O D M E N
B A S   E E R I E   R A I S A
S S S   F R O G S   S M A S H
```

84

```
A B A T   B O S O M   L A I R
D O T H   O P E R A   E L S E
J A M E S B E A R D   G I L A
S T A R T S     R R A T E D
  S N A P   I S R A E L
    J A C Q U E S P E P I N
C D L   U P S E T   S A D E
H O O P L A     D I E S E L
E R I E   N A D E R   S A L
F A N N I E F A R M E R
    C A L L A S   N E S S
I S T H M I   W I S H E S
S H E A   J U L I A C H I L D
M O R N   A F O O T   I R M A
S W I T   H O N U S   P E A K
```

85

```
C O B B   B N A I   S E E S
A U R A   R E D O   U R G E D
B R O W   I V A N   C I R C E
  A L L D A Y S U C K E R S
A D D   O L D   N E S T E D
J A W B R E A K E R S   S T E
A D A R E     M O I S T
R A Y E   S C A M P   I H O P
    T A L E R   L E O I I
C O B   T O O T S I E R O L L
O N U S E S   T N T   S S E
  M I L K C H O C O L A T E
B O L A R   N O L A   A G E D
O N E T O   O M E N   C O V E
  S T E W   R E N D   O W E N
```

86

```
D I N A H   G L U T   B O H R
E L E N A   A O N E   A L O E
S I T I N   G O O D S K A T E
K E P T   R A N   S C E N E S
    R A R A     A D D L E
M A O   I T S A B O R E
A L F   S A L M O N   G P A S
S T I C K T O O N E S G U N S
T O T O   A T R E S T   C N N
L A T H E R E D   K O S
M A S O N     A S T I
A D E S T E   O R R
J E R S E Y J O E   A B H O R
O L G A   R I N D   C E L L O
R E E L   E G A D   T R Y O N
```

87

```
S E L E S   S T R O P   J A W
O L I V E   T I A R A   E R A
S A F E C R A C K E R   W I N
O N E R   E L K E   T W E E D
    M A N E   S N E L L S
R O C O C O   P A L E S T
O H A R E   A R B O R   H O D
S I T E   S L E E T   T I N E
S O B   F E A S T   P I E C E
  U N L E S S   G O L F E R
A F R A I D     T A I L
L I G H T   S P U R   A I D A
I L L   T R A I N R O B B E R
A L A   E A G L E   A L E C K
S Y R   D E A L S   T E X A S
```

88

```
E G G S   C A G E R   T E E S
R A R E   A R U L E   E D N A
O P E C   S T R E P   Q U O D
S E E T H E   G N U   U C L A
  N I B   F L A B B I E S T
C A B O O D L E   L I L
I V A N   E O S   I T A S C A
T I C   I M P   I C E   O O M
E S K I M O   O N A   A C M E
    N S C   I G N I T I O N
P A S T O R A L E   A L A
R I T E   A R C   S M A L L S
O M A R   T E A S E   S I A M
M A G I   I N N E R   E S T E
S T E M   C A S T E   S T E W
```

89

```
  G R U B   S E V E   J A N E
A R U B A   E N I D   O X E N
C O M E S   P E R I   I L E D
C U B R E P O R T E R S
S P A   B A Y O U   A T L A S
      H O R S   O K D   A S I
A N G O R A   S S E   B L T S
B E R E N S T A I N B E A R S
O W E D   O I L   N O R W A Y
U T E   E L M   G E R M
T O N E R   E A U D E   M A I
    G R I Z Z L Y A D A M S
W A X Y   S O U L   L I N E N
A T O P   I N R E   I D O N T
T E X T   S E E D   S I N S
```

90

```
B A R R   O R A N   S C A P E
I S E E   L I M O   H A L L S
K I E V   A B O W   O N T O P
O F F O F F B R O A D W A Y
    L E V I   N U D E
L A R V A   T O D D Y   A M A
I C I E S T   R E I   S T A B
S H O R T S H O R T S T O R Y
P O T S   H O N   S C A L E S
S O S   H I M O M   O G L E S
    H E R E   E L O N
G R E A T G R E A T A U N T
F L A I R   A U K S   T H E E
A U T R Y   M E L T   E O N S
R E E S E   E D Y S   S H E S
```

91

```
S O L E   O S C A R   C R A M
P R O M   F L A R E   H A L O
C A B I N F E V E R   O D O R
A L E   A S E A   O O L I T E
    T R E K   J U D E O
A C Q U I T   P E T E R S O N
T R U S S   L O W E R   H U E
L O O K   P O L E D   F A T E
A N N   T R O L L   L U C I D
S E S S I O N S   M O N K E Y
  E N E M Y   G O L D
S A T O R I   B E L L   M A I
O C H O   S H A N T Y T O W N
D E U T   E R N I E   K O O K
A T T Y   S H E E N   O N L Y
```

92

```
H E M S   A G E S   M I C A S
O P I E   T A M E   A L A M O
D I N E   B R I M   N I N A S
  C A N T A B R I G I A N S
H U R   I T O   O L D E S T
E R E C T S   B A R A   R E O
T E T R A   P Y L E   T Y R O
    A N G E L E N O S
L I M B   A L A S   K A P P A
I S A   S T E W   R A R E L Y
P O T A T O   O O P   N A N
  L I V E R P U D L I A N S
M A N O R   A S E A   L I M E
S T E I N   A N O N   T E A R
S E E D S   R A N D   O S S A
```

93

A	T	O	M	S		E	R	G	O		H	A	S	P
L	O	P	E	S		C	O	A	L		E	T	T	A
D	O	E	S	N	T	H	O	L	D	W	A	T	E	R
O	K	R	A		Y	O	K	E		A	T	I	L	T
		A	S	A	P			S	P	L	I	C	E	S
M	O	T		M	E	A	T		E	E	N			
A	L	I	M	B		L	O	S	T		G	H	I	J
G	I	V	E	I	T	S	O	M	E	J	U	I	C	E
I	D	E	S		H	O	T	E		O	P	T	E	D
			S	P	A		H	E	R	S		T	R	I
W	A	S	H	E	R	S			O	H	O	H		
A	R	E	A	L		A	S	S	T		F	E	E	T
S	M	E	L	L	S	T	H	E	C	O	F	F	E	E
T	O	I	L		H	O	O	T		D	E	A	L	S
E	R	N	S		E	N	D	S		E	R	N	S	T

94

L	O	W	E		S	H	E	D		C	A	S	T
A	R	E	N	T		H	A	T	E		A	G	A	R
W	R	I	T	E	R	I	G	H	T		S	O	L	E
		G	R	O	O	V	E		A	A	R	O	N	
A	C	H	E		B	A	N	N	E	D	B	A	N	D
A	L	W	A	Y	S			A	S	E	A			
M	E	H	T	A		T	A	T	A		S	A	W	
E	R	E		T	H	A	I	T	I	E		E	T	A
	S	K	Y		O	I	L	Y		S	W	O	O	N
			P	E	E	N			F	E	R	U	L	E
S	T	E	A	L	S	T	E	E	L		E	L	L	S
	C	R	A	C	K		L	L	A	M	A	S		
R	I	S	K		S	T	A	L	K	S	T	O	C	K
E	P	E	E		P	A	T	E		T	H	U	L	E
W	E	L	T		A	M	E	N		S	L	U	G	

95

E	L	M	S		S	W	A	P		D	R	O	L	L
R	I	A	L		P	H	I	L		R	A	D	I	O
E	T	N	A		H	E	R	O		I	N	E	P	T
C	H	I	M	N	E	Y	S	W	I	F	T			
T	E	A	S	E	R			S	O	T		M	P	S
			W	E	E	P			T	E	R	E	S	A
A	M	A	S	S		L	O	G	A	R	I	T	H	M
L	O	N	E		S	O	L		C	R	A	M		
P	O	K	E	R	F	A	C	E		S	H	O	W	Y
H	E	L	P	E	R			H	E	A	P			
A	D	E		D	E	B		R	U	D	E	S	T	
			C	H	E	E	S	E	G	R	A	T	E	R
R	O	D	E	O		S	E	X	Y		L	U	R	E
P	R	I	N	T		O	R	A	L		E	D	G	E
M	E	E	T	S		T	A	M	E		S	E	E	D

96

R	A	G	E		A	B	A	C	U	S		C	H	E
E	M	I	L		B	R	E	A	S	T		L	A	D
B	I	N	G		B	A	R	B	A	R	A	A	N	N
A	N	N	A	M	A	Y		F	A	R	I	N	A	
	I	R	A		E	R	A		I	R	M	A	S	
O	R	E		M	A	R	Y	J	A	N	E			
R	O	M	P	E	D		E	A	R		S	L	O	W
S	T	A	R	T	E	R		R	E	S	T	I	V	E
O	L	E	O		L	E	E		T	I	S	S	U	E
			S	U	E	E	L	L	E	N		A	M	P
	R	E	M	A	N		F	L	A		G	E	M	
A	V	A	I	L	S		R	A	E	D	A	W	N	
J	O	Y	C	E	C	A	R	O	L		I	R	A	E
A	K	A		S	O	R	E	S	T		T	I	R	E
H	E	S		S	T	E	L	A	E		S	E	N	D

97

I	D	E	S		V	A	R	G	A	S		P	U	T
M	U	L	L		I	S	A	A	C	S		A	S	E
B	E	A	U	B	R	I	D	G	E	S		R	A	N
U	L	T	R	A		I	E	R		I	A	G	O	
E	S	E		B	O	R	I	S	B	E	C	K	E	R
			E	A	V	E			S	E	E			
E	R	I	N		U	M	A		A	D	E	L	E	
B	E	N	J	A	M	I	N	B	R	I	T	T	E	N
	B	O	L	O	S		C	R	O		E	S	T	E
			A	I	T			E	T	T	A			
B	O	N	N	I	E	B	L	A	I	R		Q	U	A
R	A	D	S		L	A	I		N	O	U	N	S	
I	T	E		B	A	R	B	A	R	A	B	A	C	H
D	E	R		A	N	G	E	L	O		I	S	L	E
E	S	S		A	D	E	L	I	E		S	H	E	S

98

F	O	E	S		E	G	G	S		A	B	B	O	T
I	P	S	O		S	O	R	E		L	L	A	N	O
J	E	T	S	E	T	T	E	R		L	A	N	C	E
I	C	H		R	O	H		B	R	I	C	K	E	D
			N	I	P	I	T		E	E	K			
B	A	S	I	C		C	R	O	S	S	B	A	R	
O	M	E	G	A	S		E	L	O		E	L	E	M
S	O	P	H		A	B	L	E	R		A	A	R	E
S	U	I	T		L	I	L		T	R	U	M	A	N
	R	A	S	P	U	T	I	N		A	T	O	N	E
			H	O	T		S	E	A	L	Y			
M	A	N	A	T	E	E		A	S	P		T	A	J
A	M	I	D	E		D	A	R	K	H	O	R	S	E
L	I	N	E	N		A	R	T	E		R	E	E	F
L	E	A	S	T		M	E	O	W		D	E	A	F

99

P	E	W	S		C	A	P	A		G	A	R	B	O
E	L	H	I		A	L	I	F		A	D	I	E	U
A	L	E	G		R	O	U	G	H	R	I	D	E	R
K	E	Y	H	O	L	E		H	E	L	M	E	T	S
			T	V	S		S	A	R	I				
C	L	O	S	E	B	U	T	N	O	C	I	G	A	R
H	U	T		R	A	G	U		W	O	L	E		
A	R	T	S		D	O	D	G	E		W	R	I	T
N	C	O	S		I	A	M	S		K	E	A		
T	H	I	R	T	Y	S	O	M	E	T	H	I	N	G
			E	O	N	S		R	E	O				
D	O	M	I	N	G	O		J	I	N	G	L	E	D
R	O	U	N	D	A	B	O	U	T		T	O	G	O
A	N	I	M	E		B	R	A	U		I	C	O	N
B	A	R	E	D		Y	E	N	S		E	I	N	E

100

L	A	P	P		S	H	Y		H	A	U	L	E	R
E	R	O	O		P	E	A		O	N	S	A	L	E
S	T	O	P		H	A	L		W	I	N	C	E	S
S	A	P	P	H	I	R	E	S		M	A	U	V	E
			D	A	U	N	T		T	I	A		N	E	T
A	W	E		E	X	H	A	U	S	T	F	A	N	S
L	O	C	H	S		S	P	I	E	R				
I	N	K	Y		O	A	T	E	S		E	T	A	L
			M	E	R	C	I		S	E	I	N	E	
S	P	E	N	D	T	H	R	I	F	T		R	A	G
T	U	X		A	S	E		B	L	A	S	E		
A	R	I	L	S		D	R	A	I	N	P	I	P	E
S	P	L	I	N	E		E	N	E		O	R	A	L
E	L	E	V	E	S		D	E	R		C	O	G	S
S	E	D	E	R	S		O	Z	S		K	N	E	E

PORTABLE, AFFORDABLE CROSSWORDS *from* RANDOM HOUSE

Each selection features 100 fun and easy crosswords presented in a convenient package. These puzzles are sure to delight anyone who's on the go or just on a break. Wherever you plan to be, make sure you have one of these portable volumes by your side.